"What a
gal"

THE WILD AND WAYWARD TALES OF TAMMI TRUE

by Nancy Myers and David Hopkins

To Marsha,

Tammi True

Nov 21, 2013

> David Hopkins
> P.O. Box 735
> Arlington, Texas 76004
>
> www.thatdavidhopkins.com
> www.truestuff.biz

First Printing: November 2013

ISBN 978-1-304-55746-9

Book design by Paul Milligan

Portions of this book were originally published in
D Magazine, March 2011 from "Miss Excitement:
Why Dallas Burlesque Owes a Debt to Tammi True"
by David Hopkins.

This book is based, in part, upon actual events, per-
sons, and companies. The events are portrayed to the
best of Nancy Myer's memory. Everything here is true,
but it may not be entirely factual.

"I can't give away too much.
Nobody will want my book."

—Nancy Myers

"Would you say that's stretching
a good thing too far?"

—Tammi True

Prologue

In 2010, I pitched the idea for an article on the re-emerging burlesque scene in Dallas. My editor Tim Rogers liked it, and thus I began work on my first feature for D Magazine. I initially requested that the article be 3,000 words long. Tim asked for 2,000 words. I gave him 2,755 words.

I started by interviewing Shoshana Portnoy who I went to college with. She's a show producer and an editor for Pincurl Magazine. My process was I'd interview someone—voice recorder, steno notepad, all that. Then I would go home and immediately write a story about my experience. Without any regard for the final product, I'd just jot down everything I could remember about the interview itself.

An excerpt:

We met on Saturday, October 9th at 3 pm at Libertine Bar on Greenville Avenue. When I got out of my car, Shoshana was already there, sitting on a bench outside, talking on the phone and smoking a long cigarette. When she noticed me, she greeted me with "How's your world?" to which I gave a recap of my difficulty finding a book on burlesque at Half-Price Books. Do I look in the women's studies section or sexuality in culture?

"Or I would think it might be in the theater section." She pauses. "Actually, you know why you couldn't find a book?"

She gives an answer to my problem and another drag on the cigarette. Apparently, so-and-so works there, and she snags all the books on burlesque that arrive.

"I'll talk to her and see if we can get some of those books to you."

Shoshana talks like a producer, always setting something up and making plans.

Shoshana put me in contact with almost everyone I needed for the article. That evening, I went to Teddy's Room to continue my research. The next morning, I met with Pixie O'Kneel. Pixie allowed me to sit in on a dress rehearsal for her upcoming Bewitching Burlesque production.

An excerpt:

I parked my car at the corner of South Crowdus and Canton in Deep Ellum. It was Sunday, October 10th at 10:50 am. I walked across the street to the Hub Theater. Two girls were walking in the front door, carrying various items – PVC pipe, a frilly dress, burlap cloth, a lamp, stilts, a straight jacket, and an axe.

Inside the Hub Theater, it couldn't be more different than the squeaky clean, exclusive Teddy's Room. I walked past a curtain and into the seating area of the theater. I met Pixie O'Kneel, a short woman with thick dark hair cut short. I introduced myself, and we stepped back into the lobby to talk. She introduced me to her partner Glam Amour. Contrasting in height, she towered over Pixie and myself. Pixie offered me a mimosa and muffins.

There's some girl asleep on the couch.

Back in the theater, Pixie worked with the girls, helping them with their props and set pieces. She steps away to listen to the volume of the music for the show with Tony, the sound guy.

"More or less?"
"I think right there is good?"
She listens again as the music swells.
"That's a little too much."

A few nights later, I interviewed Angi B Lovely. Afterward, I drove to Denton for the Tiki A GoGo show.

I had a lot of material, and I probably could have continued interviewing performers and attending shows, but I needed a perspective on old-school burlesque.

Shoshana put me in touch with Nancy Myers (aka Tammi True). At the time, Nancy was impossible to Google search. There wasn't any information floating around on the Internet. Surprising, since she headlined at the Carousel Club that Jack Ruby owned. I talked with her on the phone and then we met in person.

Nancy is funny, candid, and foul mouthed. The perfect interview. It turns out she hadn't done any interviews in quite a long time. Her whole life, people had been asking her about Jack Ruby. No one asked Nancy about Tammi True.

The problem I encountered was I didn't have a magazine article. I had two magazine articles: one about modern burlesque and one about Nancy. I called my editor for some guidance. He suggested one of the stories needed to be subordinate to the other. Either this is a story about modern burlesque with Tammi True as an interesting footnote or this story is about Tammi with modern burlesque as the coda (i.e., her legacy lives on). It was decided that the story needed to focus on Nancy/Tammi. Hours worth of research, interviews, and field trips on modern burlesque would go unused.

I scheduled a second interview with Nancy. I sent my finished article to Tim a week later.

After the magazine came out, I decided that 2,755 words were not nearly enough.

The Wild and Wayward Tales of Tammi True

I'm sitting with a 72-year-old woman, looking at a scrapbook filled with naked photos of her, naked with the exception of pasties and a G-string. She's smoking hot, and I'm not quite sure how to react. She turns the page in her scrapbook. There's a business card for the Carousel Club: "Offering Sophisticated, Risqué, Provocative, Delightful Entertainment—Your Host—Jack Ruby."

She smiles. "The Sixth Floor Museum wants all this stuff when I die."

In the 1960s, Nancy Powell, better known as Tammi True, headlined at the Carousel Club, the striptease venue owned by Jack Ruby. Throughout her career as a burlesque dancer, she performed in several downtown Dallas clubs and traveled the country with her routine.

They called her Miss Excitement.

Unlike some associates of Ruby's, Nancy remained reclusive, shying from interviews. She gave Esquire an interview decades ago, but felt the magazine misrepresented her. It was not easy to find her. The townhouses in her part of Grand Prairie all look the same. The address numbers are not clearly visible from the cracked street, and the lane in the housing complex weaves in an illogical pattern. Fortunately, she stood outside on her small patch of front yard. As I drove past, our eyes met and I knew it was her. I stopped the car, introduced myself.

A few minutes later, I'm in her living room, digging through the contents of a large plastic bin filled with scrapbooks, old newspapers, playbills, and pocket guides to Dallas entertainment. Inside her house, she has a poodle and a cat she named PITA ("pain in the ass"). A finished newspaper crossword puzzle sits folded in half on her coffee table and nearby on a bookshelf there is a crossword puzzle dictionary. There are framed photos, antiques, numerous plants, and crafted knick-knacks. It looks like any grandmother's home. No one would suspect her former life.

**

"All I know prior to when I was born is what I was told by my grandmother. My mother got pregnant when she was 15, because she had met this young man. My uncle had a gambling casino in the basement of the Westbrook Hotel in downtown Fort Worth.

That was my father's brother. He was a high-roller. They were from Bowie, Texas. My father had come down here, and he was living with his brother who had the casino. That is back when gambling was still legal. He was a high-roller, and my father, apparently, was driving around in a new car. He had a car, dressed snappy, two-tone shoes and all that crap. I'm sure that's what got my mother in trouble because they were so poor. My grandmother worked at the WPA. She thought that was going to be her ticket out.

They probably met downtown somewhere. Downtown used to be the place to go for shopping or whatever. I imagine she met him downtown, and he just won her over. I don't know whether it was in the back seat of a car or whether he took her to a hotel. I don't know. She just made a V shape and vibrated when she shouldn't have and here I am.

He was 18, 19. I don't know. My mother met him when she was 15. She got pregnant. Well, guess what? Uncle and family didn't want any part of me. They sent him off and made him join the Navy. He was on a ship when I born. That's the story my grandmother told me.

This young man married my mother not long before I was born, like two or three months before I was born. He was a friend of my mother's brother, and he liked my mother a lot. He asked her to marry him. My grandmother thought that was a great idea, because back then, most families sent their kids away. Grandmother couldn't afford that.

My mother told him she would, but she wanted me to have my real father's name. He agreed to that. They got married two or three

months before I was born. His name was
Monroe Owens."

**

David: On your birth certificate, it would be
Nancy Owens?

Nancy: No. Bolen.

David: Bolen?

Nancy: My father's name was Neil Douglas
Bolen.

David: You were born Nancy Bolen?

Nancy: Yeah.

David: What's your middle name?

Nancy: Monnell. My stepfather's name was
Monroe, and my mother's name was Margie Nell.
She put Mon and Nell together. She probably did
that because she had insisted on giving me my real
daddy's last name. I don't know if he's my real
daddy or not, but that supposedly was my real
father. Unusual, isn't it?

David: It is.

Nancy: I was named after my grandmother, too. Her name was Nancy Idella Jones. My grandfather's name was George Washington Jones.

David: Your stepfather, his name again?

Nancy: Monroe Owens.

David: Do you remember your real father's brother's name?

Nancy: The uncle that had the gambling casino, his name was Forrest Bolen. He had another brother. His name was IT Bolen. He was a drunk. He was the black sheep of the family. We'd see him downtown, and he was always friendly. He liked me a lot. I don't remember interacting at all with Forrest, the older brother.

David: You were born in Fort Worth?

Nancy: Saint Joseph's Hospital in Fort Worth, Texas.

**

"Neil was like any other boy. I'm sure his brother, my uncle, was not real thrilled about it. They got him to join the Navy, got him in the service right away, and he was shipped off somewhere. He left my mother holding the bag, just like most boys do. It's all I know.

The story my grandmother and mother made

up was that they ran off and got married. When my grandmother and my uncle found out what they had done, they had it annulled because they were too young.

My uncle made my dad join the service to keep them apart. After my dad had gone off to the Navy, my mother found out she was pregnant and it was too late to do anything. He was on a ship somewhere. I believed that. It sounded logical to me.

My mother, all those years when I was growing up, she would dial his number and have me talk to him. I called him Daddy because I knew that Monroe was not my real father."

**

"I was an only child. My real father never had any other children. And years later, when I was in my late 30s or 40s—my mother passed away when I was about 36—I used to call my daddy every now and then. As the years wore on, he got more receptive to me being his kid. He asked about my mother.

'She passed away,' I said.

He was upset I didn't call him to let him know. I'm thinking, 'Why in the hell would you want to know? All these years, and you never...'

He said something about how he was all alone, and didn't have any family.

'You could have had a family,' I said, 'but you chose not to. It's too late now.'

I had a confrontation with him in my early 20s.

One day, my girlfriend saw him downtown. She was one of my best friends. She said something to him about 'your daughter Nancy.' He said, 'That bitch isn't anything to me.'

She told me what he said.

I was out one night in a club. He was there. He needed to go somewhere. He asked me if I would take him, and I told him, 'No.'

'If you want me to be your daddy,' he said. 'I'll be your daddy.'

I just looked at him and I said, 'If I was going to pick a daddy, it would be somebody a hell of a lot better than you.'

He was cocky. Occasionally, I would call him to check up. I'm sure he's passed away by now. He wasn't much of a father."

**

"My stepfather went to war, and that's when my mother started drinking. I don't think my mother ever got over my father, if you want to know the truth. Him dumping her like that.

Monroe went to war after Pearl Harbor. He was in the cavalry.

I always knew he just my stepfather, but I was crazy about him. He was good to me, and he never had any other children. Even after he and my mother divorced, he never had any children. I remember how good looking he was when he came home on leave. He had on his uniform, and those tall boots like the Aggies wear, I'm like, 'Holy!' He was dark-headed and brown-eyed, handsome.

I remember the President on the radio when they bombed Pearl Harbor, because of my grandmother saying, 'Shh! Be quiet!'

Monroe made it through the war, but he was right in the middle of the bad stuff. He was on the ground. He saw some of the concentration camps, and the bodies. I'm sure it was hard on him."

Monroe and Nancy's mother got a divorce when Nancy was seven years old.

**

"My mother became a full-blown alcoholic while he was gone. Every day, she'd take me with her to the neighborhood bars. There were two neighborhood bars. One of them was called Cactus Inn, and the other one was Indian's Saloon, down the street on South Main, within walking distance of our house, because we didn't have a car.

She'd take me with her, and I was precocious. I spent most of my time with adults when I was a kid, because I didn't have any brothers or sisters to play with. My grandmother kept me locked in because she was afraid something bad might happen to me if I went down the street.

I was bad about running off. If got a chance, I'd run down the street to find some kids to play with. It's during the war, and they were playing all that wartime music. The boogie-woogie came out. I remember dancing in these bars to the boogie-woogie. Guys would give me money for dancing."

**

"When I knew my ass was in a crack, I always tried to be cute to not get an ass whipping. Sometimes it worked, most of the time it didn't. I was an only child. I was so lonely. I didn't have anybody to play with, and my grandmother was protective.

She had three damn hooks on the screen door. Since we didn't have air conditioning, we always had our doors and windows open. My grandmother had put three locks, one on the top, one where they always go in the middle, and then one down.

My mother would make me lie down and take a nap during the day. When she went to sleep, I'd get up, get the broom, and unlatch the locks. I'd undo that top one, and that middle one, and I'd sneak out.

One day, there was a girl who lived down about half a block down from where we lived. Her name was Sally. I went down to her house, because I wanted to play. Back then, these people would come around neighborhoods with a Shetland pony, chaps and a little cowboy hat, and take pictures of kids. Kind of like the ice cream man, but they would take pictures of the kids.

He had stopped at Sally's house. I saw my mother coming. I told them 'I want my picture made! I want my picture made!' He set me up on the pony. I'm sitting up there looking cute, and I thought, 'Boy, this is going to save me.' She bought the picture, but she still whipped my ass!

I learned that I was cute, people liked me, and I could get away with stuff more than other kids could.

People who have a hard time growing up, they use humor to cope. Most comedians will tell you their childhood was kind of tough. They were either too fat in school, or a geek or a nerd. In order to deal with all that, you have to act like everything's great. A lot of that comes from the way you're raised."

**

"They had one black radio station, KNOK, in Fort Worth. I was playing with the radio one day and I hit it. I went, 'Oh man, I like that music.' I started playing that. My mother would sigh, and say, 'What are you doing?' I loved it.

They played blues. They called it rhythm and blues back then. That was in the '50s. I had an old bitty turntable, cheap, made out of cardboard. I started buying records. I had 'Lawdy Miss Clawdy.' Lloyd Price did that. Who was that other guy I had? T Bone Walker. I had a bunch of that music. My mother thought I'd lost my mind.

I wasn't crazy about Elvis. When he started, I thought he was funny. When I saw him on TV, and he was doing all that hip stuff, I thought he looked like a spastic. I didn't like his music until after he got out of the service. His voice changed and mellowed out. That's when I liked him. He came to Fort Worth in his pink Cadillac. I wasn't even interested enough to try to go see him. I probably thought I was more grown up than all those other teenage girls. Screaming, hollering, fainting. I was too grown up for all that silly shit."

**

"My mom was not ever like a mom. She was a happy time person. When she was drunk, she was real happy. She wasn't a mean drunk or anything. As a matter of fact, she was a lot of fun when she was drunk, because she'd let me do a lot more. She was always more like my sister. I remember we'd be playing around and she'd tell me, 'You need to go away. You're getting on my nerves.' I remember that a lot. But we would go to the movies together. She took me to see the Mummy or Wolf Man.

That one night, we were playing in bed. I slept with her and I heard this sound...

'What is that?'

She was scratching on the sheet. She scared the hell out of me. She liked to do that. She was kind of fun.

Then she got fat, and I was kind of embarrassed about her being so fat. That's when she started hitting the bottle pretty heavy. It was okay, because she took me to the bars with her. I was just three, four years old.

They'd play the jukebox, and I'd dance. All the other drunks liked me. I became Miss Betty Grable, 'Introducing Miss Betty Grable.'

I loved her because she was my mother, but she was not. I don't know how to describe my relationship with her. I never hated her or anything.

It was just like she was a sister, or something. She disciplined me some, too. She gave me spankings, but my grandmother was always the main disciplinarian. She ran the house."

**

"My grandmother converted to Catholicism when my mother was 11 or 12. We have a cathedral in Fort Worth called St. Patrick's. Right next door is the Catholic school, St. Ignatius. My grandmother got a job in the kitchen at St. Ignatius. She decided to convert, and had my mother baptized. When I was six weeks old, the bishop baptized me. That's all I ever knew growing up. I always felt I was okay with that, being a Catholic. I don't think I want to be anything else. I took a lot of jokes for being a Catholic, too. Yeah, I worship idols."

**

"I received my first communion at Saint Mary's. I got expelled from Our Lady of Victory in the second grade. That should be a record.

Our Lady of Victory was a big Catholic School on Hemphill Street. That's where I was going to school, and it was Halloween. I rode the bus, because the bus ran right in front of our house. I had to ride the bus, because that was too far to walk. I had a bus card. It was pink. And when you'd ride the bus, they'd punch it. It had like about 20 rides on it, and you could buy it in advance. My grandmother would buy that, and I could hand him my card, and he'd punch it. I'd ride the public bus. They didn't have school buses. I rode the bus to school.

It was Halloween. We had a little Halloween party.

This little girl that was a friend of mine, she wanted to go home with me. I said, 'Sure.' She got on the bus and went home with me.

When it was five o'clock, my grandmother asked her about going home. She didn't know her address. She didn't know her phone number.

I don't know how my grandmother found out how to get in touch with her parents, but anyways she did.

They were at a party at the Country Club, or somewhere. They had money, and we didn't. They had to come get her. They were pissed.

They expelled me. I don't know if they were

big contributors or what, but anyway, I became the bad person there. I was the underdog. I had lured her away from school. They expelled me from Our Lady of Victory.

They had built a church behind the church, St. Mary's. I went there."

**

"I was running wild while my grandmother was at work. That summer, my aunt lived in Dallas. She came over, got me, and took me over to Dallas for a week, just to spend some time with her. I wanted to come back home. I waited until she was asleep one day. I stole $2 out of her purse. I went out the window. I was seven. I got on the bus and I rode the bus to the streetcar line. That's back when Dallas still had streetcars. I transferred to a streetcar and told the streetcar driver that I needed to get off at the bus station, Greyhound bus station. He let me off downtown and told me just to walk over there, where he showed me and told me where it was.

I walked in there. I walked up to the counter, and I said, 'I need a half fare, one way, to Fort Worth.'

It cost 40 cents. They gave me a ticket. I got on the damn bus, and I went home. When I got home, got off the bus in downtown Fort Worth, I thought, 'I'm in big trouble.' I was scared to go home.

I went into the New Liberty Theater right

there at 10th, right off Main Street. They always had a double feature. I stayed in the movie until I don't know what time. It was dark.

I had popcorn and all that stuff, too, because I had two whole dollars. Finally, I went home. We lived on the other side of the viaduct there on Main Street by the old train station where the train went across.

There was a tunnel through there. I would stop on this end if it was dark, because I was afraid somebody might be hiding behind those posts somewhere. I'd take a deep breath and I'd run like hell to get through it to the other side. We lived on the corner in an apartment.

I went home, and I was in big trouble. They were scared to death, and not only that, my uncle was a policeman in Dallas, my aunt's husband. They had the entire police department looking for me. After that incident, my grandmother decided I needed to be someplace safe.

My grandmother worked at Saint Joseph's Hospital. There was an order of nuns, Sisters of Saint Joseph, who ran the hospital. They had this sister orphanage called Saint Joseph's Home for Girls in Dallas. She had been talking. They all knew the situation, because I used to go there after school. One of the nuns helped me with my homework. And then the other one, I'd go to the kitchen, she'd feed me. I'd lie down in the cloakroom on a little cot until my grandmother got off. She worked 3 to 11.

They were all aware of the situation that my

mother was a drunk. My grandmother was worried something was going to happen to me. They made arrangements to get me in at Saint Joseph's Home for Girls in Dallas. It was awful. I'd look in the mirror, and I would pinch myself. 'This can't be real.'

One Sunday a month, we had visitors. My grandmother came every time. I was there four years, and I never saw my mother.

I got out in 1950, and I was 12. I turned 12 that summer."

**

"My mother was a person that never found herself. All her life, she was dependent on someone else for a place to live, and all that. It was always my grandmother. She would move out sometimes, and she would always move back in. Right after I came home from school she had married a man, Bob Fore. He was a great guy. He made a terrific stepfather. I went and lived with them for a while, because she had sobered up. They had rented a house. They had a car.

I lived with them quite a bit. He had kids somewhere else, and he got picked up at work for back child support. They took him off down to south Texas somewhere. He never came back. My mother and I were back with my grandmother.

I've never been anything like her. I made up my mind I was not going to be a drunk, and I was not going to go through my life depending on somebody else, and whatever they felt at the moment.

Nobody was going to be able to tell me to get out, or threaten me that, 'I pay the bills, and you do what I say...' My grandmother would do that with her. Jump over her for being drunk, and coming in drunk. She would talk down to her. Nobody's ever going to do that to me.

I became a lot stronger than my mother. My mother was a weak person. I don't see any similarities, other than she had a great fun-loving personality."

**

"When I found out my real daddy had abandoned my mom and didn't want to have anything to do with me, I felt stupid. My grandmother, one night we were just talking and she told me. I felt stupid about calling him all those years and talking to him and calling him 'Daddy' when the man obviously did not want to have anything to do with me.

My world turned upside down, and I went ape. I thought I'm not only poor, but I'm a bastard and I'm not as good as all these other kids at school. I started hanging out with—I'm not going to say bad—but the rejects. There's always this clique and then there's these other kids. They accepted me. One thing led to another.

My grandmother was so damn strict. I would sneak out and go to the park show. They had these park shows on Friday nights at the local neighborhood parks. They would put up a screen. Kids would go and take blankets and snacks. We'd socialize and watch the movie, some of it. I'd want to go to that.

'No.'

I'd say, 'Why?'

'Because.'

'Because why?'

'Because I said so.'

I hated that.

Converted Catholics are stricter than the ones who are born into it. They're like born again Christians or people that have quit smoking. They've got to go way to the other side. She was strict. I got to the point, well, I'll just do it anyway. I'd take off. As I progressed, if I took off with a friend, I'd be afraid to go home. I'd go home with a friend. They'd be calling the police and have the police looking for me. I got tangled up in the juvenile court system and had a caseworker and all kinds of crap.

My grandma's telling them I can't do anything with her, she's incorrigible, you all need to send her to reform school and they did. I was 15 and they sent me off to Gainesville.

First thing I did was try to run. They called me Rabbit. That was my nickname. I was fast. Even the police called me Rabbit because a few times they'd see me and try to get me and I'd haul ass and they couldn't catch me.

I didn't get far. They immediately put my butt

in the discipline cottage, which was called MacAnally. It didn't have bars, but it had grates on the window. There was a mattress on the floor with a sheet. It was like being in solitary confinement almost. I could have books. I could read.

They had land where they grew things. They had cantaloupes. They put me out there working in the cantaloupe patch. I got sunburned badly. It was so bad I could just take and pull sheets of skin off. They couldn't put me out to work. I'm lying on my stomach on this mattress and they're putting Noxzema on my back every so often.

I had to stay there. I got 30 days, but I only stayed about 20. They put me in a cottage with the worst girls. I decided if I'm going to be here, then I need to get back in school. Actually, I ended up in the honor cottage.

In honor cottage, I could come and go. I just had to sign out and sign back in. I had a teacher who liked me. She would take me home with her, and I could spend the weekend. I took tennis lessons. I took business. I got my diploma and all my certifications, typing and shorthand. The only thing I remember with shorthand to write is 'dear sir' and 'I am.'

I typed 71 words a minute. I was a certified typist. I did real well in that. I was second in the class. I did all that and got through it. I could have gone home sooner, but if I did then I wouldn't have finished school. I stayed two or three months longer than I had to, so I could go ahead and finish school. By then, I was in honor cottage and I could come and go. It was okay.

The courts were tough on kids back then, not like they are now. The person who had been over the juvenile department that worked with incorrigibles, he became a judge. His name was Lynn Ross. I went to see him after I grew up. He told me he was proud of me because I had turned my life around."

**

Nancy found a boyfriend at the nearby Carswell Air Force Base. Nancy was young, but ready to start her life.

"My boyfriend Chuck and I had a big fight. And then, me and my grandmother had a big fight. She was always on Chuck's side. I was angry with him because when I got out of school, he had bought me an engagement ring. I told him that I was ready to get married right then.

He said to me, 'Your grandmother and I have talked about this and we think that you and I should wait.'

'Well, then maybe you should marry my grandmother,' I said.

I threw his ring at him. My grandmother was mad. She told me to get my ass out because I was mean to Chuck. Cecil called and I told him that my grandmother was kicking me out.

'Don't worry,' he said. 'I'll come get you,' which he did. We were together for the next five years."

Nancy takes a drag from her cigarette, shakes her head.

"Cecil Powell, my savior."

**

David: When was your first marriage?

Nancy: In '50... when did I get married, '55? Yeah, '55.

David: Let me write that down.

Nancy: I think it was. I'll have to stop and think on that. I got out of school in '54. I did have a double promotion somewhere along the line. I got out of school early.

David: About how old were you at the time?

Nancy: I was 17. Is that right? 17?

**

"I don't even remember where we got married. We didn't get married in Fort Worth because I wasn't 18. My grandmother damn sure wasn't going to sign. I don't know whether we went to Oklahoma or some other place where you could get one of those little quickie marriage things. It didn't matter how old you were. They used to do that in Weatherford. Justice of the Peace would marry in the middle of the night, or the wee-hours of the morning, or whatever."

**

Cecil Powell was a burglar. "Cecil was probably the best safe man in town," Nancy recalls with a sense of pride. "That was fun and exciting, until I got pregnant."

**

"I thought I was grown, but I really grew up when I was pregnant with Dawn. When she started moving around, I realized I was having a baby. I was going to be responsible for this child. That's when I started growing up. I'd go with Cecil to the bars and hang out. He never drank a lot. He didn't do drugs or anything. He liked to hang out, drink a beer, and shoot pool, and bullshit with all of his buddies. I would go with him, and I started realizing that we were having a baby.

Things can be like that. I got to where I didn't want to go. I wanted him to stay home and work. Let's be prepared. He got to where he would just go without me. He'd know he was going to be in trouble. He's like a kid afraid to go home, because they know how much trouble they're in. It may be a day or two later, before I saw him."

**

"The FBI had charged Cecil with a crime. And they were looking for him. His sister and brother-in-law had moved to California. He decided we were going to take off and go to California.

We loaded our car and Dawn. I had her already. She was about three months old. And we got in our car and drove to California to his sister and brother-in-law's.

He got a job out there. We were living under an alias. I was there about six months. And I wanted to come home because I had never been away from home before. And I was lonesome. I missed my family. I missed all my friends.

My birthday was coming up. And he asked me what I wanted for my birthday. I said I wanted to a ticket back to Texas. For my birthday, he gave me a bus ticket for me and Dawn. I don't think he thought I'd use it, but I did.

Dawn and I got on the Greyhound bus and came back to Texas. The bus was full. I was smart enough to bring a pillow. I held her in my lap most of the way from California to El Paso.

In El Paso, some people got off and there was a black boy sitting across the aisle with an empty seat beside him. Dawn was asleep. I put her down gently in my seat. I went over and sat next to that black boy. Scared him to death, because back then you just didn't do that.

Blacks didn't sit with whites. He was up as far as he could get to the side of the bus by the window. I felt bad so I started talking to him. He was coming home on leave. I made him more comfortable. But it scared the hell out of him. I was never prejudice or anything. I didn't even think about it. I moved across the aisle and plopped down in that seat beside him. I was tired of holding that kid by the time we got to El Paso.

The FBI found out someway where Cecil was. They went into his sister's house and arrested him. They extradited him, brought him back to Fort Worth, because he fled to avoid prosecution on top of the other charges."

**

With their on-again, off-again relationship, I had difficulty keeping track of Nancy and Cecil. Sometimes they were together. Sometimes they were apart. Two years after Dawn was born, Nancy was pregnant again.

"If I was sitting, you wouldn't even know I was pregnant. I went out one time with my girl friend. Cecil and I were separated, and I was pregnant. We were sitting at the table. This guy came up and asked me to dance.

'I don't think you want to dance with me,' I said.

'Why not?'

'Because I'm pregnant.'

'Oh! That's okay, I don't mind.'

'It's okay. You don't have to dance with me.'

From behind, I didn't look pregnant or anything, because I didn't gain a lot of weight. I didn't ever gain over 15 pounds, either time I was pregnant. I carried high. I felt great when I was pregnant the first time. I was miserable when I was pregnant the second time, because Asshole wasn't helping me.

With Dawn, everything was okay, pretty much. We got lucky with her, because he had gone to work and the company he went to work for changed insurance. He was automatically covered. He'd only been there a month or so. He was automatically covered when they flipped over to the new insurance. It paid for everything, which wasn't that much. It cost $150 for my doctor and delivery."

**

David: Can you tell me about the time you tried to shoot Cecil?

Nancy: Which time?

**

"I was pregnant with Tracy. Cecil wasn't helping me, and I couldn't get a job. Back then, they wouldn't hire you if you were pregnant. And if they did hire you, they didn't have maternity benefits. I was trying to find Cecil, because I needed some help with Dawn. I knew who he was hanging out with, and somebody gave me the phone number. I called over there and I asked for him. I could hear them mumbling, putting their hand over the phone.

Whoever answered the phone said, 'He's not here.'

'He better get on the phone,' I said. 'I don't want to have to come over there.'

'You better not come over here. I'll shoot your ass.'

'Well get ready,' I said, 'because I'm coming over there.'

I hung up the phone.

I knew where the apartment was, and I knew they were lying. That night, I drove over to the apartment. I had a friend who left the back door open for me. I walked in. I came in through the kitchen. I walked into the living room. Cecil and his girl were lying asleep on a couch that made a bed.

I wanted him to know I shot him. I went over and poked him with the gun, and then backed up. He didn't move, but she sat up in the bed. As she did, she pulled the covers up to her head and lay back down. And I fired. And I shot half her ear off.

When he got up, stumbling around like he was half asleep, I tried to shoot him but the gun had jammed. He took the gun away from me. And I ran. I ran out the back door and got in my car. He came out as I was pulling off, and he opened the door and jumped in my car. We went over to my girlfriend's house. He got out and went in, and he had the gun.

'I can't believe she only bought one bullet,' he told her.

'She didn't buy one bullet. She bought nine bullets.'

He checked the gun, and he said, 'oh god.'

He had a friend come get him. They got arrested down the street. He got charged with carrying a gun as an ex-convict. Everyone who was in that apartment went to jail except me.

I was desperate. I had no income. I was staying with my grandmother, and she wasn't working. It was awful trying to buy food for Dawn. I already told my lawyer I was going to shoot Cecil if he didn't help out. I called my lawyer again that night.

'This is Nancy, and I did it.'

'Where are you?'

I told him.

'You stay there,' he said. 'In the morning, I'm going to come by and pick you up, and take you down to the jail to surrender.'

I called my mother too to let her know what I'd done. I figured the police would be by my house. They were there when I called her. They wanted me to tell them where I was. I wouldn't.

My lawyer came the next morning and got me. Took me down to the police station. I went back to the detectives and got questioned. They had taken that girl to the hospital and patched her up, and taken her to jail too, because she was a known whatever.

Cecil was in jail.

They wanted to know why I did it. I told them. They said, 'That girl's 17 years old.' Her parents were there. They went out and talked to her parents. The parents didn't want to press charges. They never booked me or anything. They just let me go home. The front page of the paper was 'Love Triangle' blah, blah, blah.

That was that time."

**

"With my second child, I was about three or four months pregnant before I even got to the doctor. We didn't have any insurance or money or anything. I went to see the doctor at least once a month. Toward the end, I was going in every week. I worked a half a day on Wednesday. I went to the doctor and took the rest of the day off.

One day, I got up and I needed to run to the store and get some gowns, because I didn't have any. My mother's friend took me over to this little shopping center

I started having pains. I'd stop and hold on to the counter. Finally, we got back and she told my mother, she said, 'She's scaring me to death.' I went in, and I said, 'I'm going to go take a bath.'

I went in there and took a bath, and when I came out the pain hit me, boom. I had this big pain and fell down on the bed. I was hurting, and Betty, my girlfriend, she was going to come and take me to the hospital.

I didn't even know where Cecil was.

'I'm not taking you,' Betty said. 'I'm calling an ambulance.'

'Tell them it's not an emergency. Don't turn the siren on,' I said.

They came and they loaded me up. She jumped up there with the driver.

A young kid was in the back of the ambulance with me, and I could tell, he was like, 'Oh, my god. I hope she doesn't have this baby before we get there.' About halfway there, they turned the siren on. Betty told them, 'Turn that siren on, I have never ridden in an ambulance with the siren on.'

They took me in and they took me upstairs. Betty was downstairs telling them, 'Oh, yeah. They've got insurance.' I didn't have any insurance with my second daughter Tracy. 'She's got insurance, but I just have to get in touch with her husband to find out.'

I waited, because I wanted to be to a point where they couldn't refuse me. She was born within the hour, by the time Betty got upstairs. I was already in the labor room; it was a done deal.

It was close."

**

The cat and mouse game between Cecil and the Law meant that Nancy had a close relationship with the police. They knew her, and she knew them. And occasionally, they could help her.

"One morning, a couple detectives were coming on duty, and I heard one of them say, 'Cecil must be in jail, again. There's Nancy sitting there.'

I'd made friends with Lieutenant George Hawkins, and he liked me a lot. I told him Cecil wasn't helping me. I didn't know where he was.

'You call me when you have that baby," he said.

I called him.

Hawkins was asking me what it was and all that. The next morning, at the hospital, they brought a free newspaper around to everybody. I opened the newspaper. There was a picture of Cecil and some of his cronies. They had all been arrested at a motel, out there on Jacksboro Highway.

Later that day, Cecil showed up at the hospital. His friend told me later, he said, 'We got arrested out there, went down and Lieutenant Hawkins was asking Cecil if he'd had the baby yet.'

'Oh, no,' Cecil said. 'I haven't had the baby.'

Hawkins looked at him and he said, 'You sorry SOB. She's had that baby. You need to get up to that hospital and pay the hospital bill, and if you don't, do you see this?'

He had big shoes, like size 14 feet. He said, 'Do you see this? I'm going to stick it up your ass.'

Cecil said, 'Yes, sir.'

He'd had him arrested and told him to get up there. He did, he came up there, but I was embarrassed. I was in a semi private room, and I'm looking over there at that girl and I think, 'Oh, god. I hope she didn't put two and two together here.'

Cecil came up and he paid. He paid enough
on the hospital bill to get me released and all that.
He took me and the baby home. He left, because
he wasn't welcome in my grandmother's house.

Cecil had accused me of it not being his, and
she looks exactly like him. Exactly. Looks like she
was picked out of his ass with a pair of tweezers."

**

"The few times that we managed to rent an
apartment and get out on our own, he would quit
work and we wouldn't have the money to pay the
utility bills or the rent. We had to sneak out and
move out in the middle of the night. I got tired of
living like that."

**

"Honey, I had Dawn when I was 18, and I
was 20 when I had Tracy, my other daughter. Bad
as Cecil was, at least I had a husband, although he
wasn't a good provider.

We divorced in 1960. Cecil and I were back
and forth, back and forth for five years. I was either living with my grandmother or his mother."

**

"Cecil left. He took off. He got him a girlfriend. They got married, and they moved to Cali-

fornia. We didn't see him for six years. I never hated him. I just wanted him to go away and leave me alone. Six years later , I picked up the phone one day and it was him. I was stunned.

Cecil told me he was in California, at first. We kept talking, and he finally admitted he and his wife had split up and gotten a divorce. He had come back home to his momma's. He wanted to know if he could see the kids.

'I don't want to get in trouble for child support,' he said.

'As long as you don't disrupt our lives, because our lives are okay without you in the picture, then I don't want the child support. You can't take them off. You have to visit them here.'

We set a date and, god, it was so sad. My youngest one didn't remember him. She was two and she just didn't remember him. Dawn remembered him a little bit, because she was four when he left.

I got them ready and I said, we'll cookout hot dogs. They were excited that they were going to get to see their daddy, but they were nervous. Dawn came in there and she was tearing up.

'I don't know what I'm going to say or what I'm going to do when he comes,' she said.

'Don't worry about it. Be yourself.'

Anyway he came and I had to go away from them, because my heart was breaking. I was crying. I started crying, because I knew they were upset and didn't know what to expect.

When he got there, I had to go back in the

house. Wherever they were, I had to go to the other spot, and it just broke my heart. But it worked out okay.

I never talked bad about him. I'm sure my grandmother did and my mother, because they didn't like him around the kids. But I never did talk bad about him. I always told them that he loved them. He just didn't want to help me take care of them.

I started letting him take them away from the house when I felt comfortable that he wasn't going to run off with them. He'd call and he'd say, 'I want to take the kids out to Casino Beach swimming. I'll pick them up so-and-so time on so-and-so day.'

I'd get them dressed and get them ready. They'd sit there and they'd wait and wait. He didn't show up.

One day he did that. He'd done it a couple of times already. I was pissed. I went out and I sat down on the porch. Dawn came out and she sat down beside me on the step.

'You know Mommy,' Dawn said. 'Daddy's not very good at keeping his promises.'

'That's exactly why I divorced him,' I said, 'and I don't love him.'

She figured it out for herself.

That's just the way he was. He had good intention, but if something else came along, like one of his friends called and said, 'Let's go shoot pool or let's go do this,' it just totally went away. He did me that way. He was just totally inconsiderate and irresponsible.

Cecil wasn't ready to settle down and take on the responsibility. I kept thinking I could get him to change, and that didn't happen. He'd promise. I'd leave and go to my grandmother's, and he'd send flowers, and call me, and 'I won't do that again.' Then, his friends would go by where he was working, and he'd walk off the job, and go with them. He was worthless. I was scared to be by myself with two children. I was just petrified. One day, I realized he wasn't helping me anyway. What did I need him for? I said, 'That's it.' "

**

"Cecil is totally different now. He's considerate now and does what he says he's going to do. I think it's just that he got so old that he couldn't do shit. All of his old friends were dying off on him—his old buddies that he'd been hanging out with ever since they were in school together.

Cecil lived with his mother. He took care of her. I give him credit for that. He was good to his mother. Then she passed away and he's out on his own. Now I'm it. We've been divorced 50 something years. Every day he calls me at least once, maybe twice. If he's got a pain anywhere, he's on the phone. 'Nancy, my stomach is hurting me bad.'

I think all the time that I'm glad I divorced him. But here he is. He was over here, and he was going on. I said, 'Maybe I ought to finish what I

started fifty years ago and put you out of your
damn misery.'

Lucky for him I raised his children to respect
their father, regardless."

There was some reason why you cared about
this person, and to me, that's sad. That you care
about somebody so much, and you had children
with them, and then you feel indifferent, or you're
just mean. That's sad. I don't know. Life's weird
isn't it?"

**

"Between '60, '61, the roller derby was in
town. They were skating out at the Northside
Coliseum, arena, whatever. There was a club
downtown Fort Worth called the Cellar, and it
was open all night long. It was like a coffee house
and this friend of mine had opened it up back in
the '50s, late '50s. You went downstairs into a cellar, a basement, and they had cushions, old cushions off of couches all on the floor and coffee
tables. There were no tables, chairs.

Everybody sat in the floor and everybody
came there after hours because they were open. I
had sunglasses so when I came out in the morning, I could put my sunglasses on.

Some of these people from the roller derby
started coming in down there. I met this guy. His
name was David Battersby.

Good-looking guy, and he was playing the bad
guy. He had his hair bleached blond and his thing

was 'Don't touch my hair.' Kind of like Gorgeous George.

We started going out. I don't know why or how, but anyway, he wanted to get married. And all his buddies, roller derby buddies, they were all friends with each other. They had two teams that were supposed to hate each other, but it's like wrestling. They all thought Dave and I should get married.

We went to Weatherford, and we got married.

All of a sudden, their roller derby deal was over. He started talking about me moving back to Queens, New York, with him. Their offices are out in Bakersfield, California, but he lived in Queens. That's where he was from. He starts talking about me and the kids moving to New York.

'I am not going to New York.' I told him, 'No. That isn't going to happen.'

So he left. We were married maybe two, three weeks. Not long at all. He left town.

I got this card in the mail. It had a picture of a guy on the front with a big knife sticking in his back. When I opened it up, it said, 'It's been a pleasure doing business with you.'

He told me he was going to have it annulled.

When I got engaged to my second husband seven or eight years later, I'm thinking, I better make sure that I'm not still married.

I called Bakersfield, and told them I needed to get in touch with Dave Battersby.

'We can give him a message.'

'Tell him Nancy Battersby's calling. His wife.'

'Oh, okay.'

In a little while, I got a phone call. It was Dave.

'I'm going to get married,' I said, 'and I just want to be sure our marriage was annulled.'

'I was afraid you were calling wanting to get back together. I'm remarried and we just had a baby.'

'Good. I just want to be sure I'm not a bigamist.'

'Oh no, I had that annulled.'

Damn, he was thinking I wanted to get back together."

**

Nancy liked to go out dancing. She met Guy Parnell from Carswell Air Force Base. He had a band. The twist was a popular dance craze, and the band wanted Nancy to dance for them. The club that booked them, however, wanted a striptease dancer. Parnell urged Nancy to try it.

"I said, 'I cannot do that.' I was raised Catholic. I was kind of a moral immoral bitch back then. He thought I'd be great, and then they'd book them."

Nancy's friend Elizabeth Klug also encouraged her and offered to make her a dress.

" 'I'll make you a costume,' she said. We bought some green satin and green sequins—a bra, panties, and a short dress. We didn't know anything about breakaway zippers. She put hooks and eyes all the way down the side of this little dress that she made."

Jimmy Levens, the owner of the Skyliner Ballroom on Jacksboro Highway, saw her dance. His club did striptease on Friday and Saturday nights. Sherry Lynn, a stripper from Dallas who worked at the Skyliner, offered to train her. Lynn told her to just dance, and then she would cue Nancy when to take something off.

"I just couldn't do it," Nancy says. "They kept pushing me out. I made it. When I got through, she agreed with Jimmy that I had a lot of talent. She took me under her wing."

Nancy danced at the Skyliner on Fridays and Saturdays under the stage name Tammi True. She made $50 for both nights. In contrast, she made $35 a week at her day job. Nancy was ready to make her weekend side project a full-time affair.

**

"I just picked out the name 'Tammi' for no reason. The lady that was booking me in Fort Worth, she said why don't you call yourself Tammi True, because of the movie *Tammy Tell Me True* with Sandra Dee. I said okay. That's fine.

I'd seen it. It was a real popular movie. She might have made a couple of those Tammy movies. Everybody knew it."

The playful irony wouldn't be missed on anybody. Sandra Dee was such an innocent girl—while Nancy's stage persona was no Sandra Dee.

**

"I decided a long time ago that I didn't have to lie to anybody about anything. I went in and told my grandmother that I had been offered a job as a striptease dancer. She looked at me.

'It's not against the law, is it?' she asked.

'No.'

'You can do what you've got to do.'

I was kind of shocked about that. I think my grandmother was probably the madam of a whorehouse when she was young.

She made bathtub gin out in West Texas. She ran a boarding house. I don't know that for a fact, but she was pretty wise and I'm thinking 'hmm.' "

**

"Jacksboro Highway was rough. It was where the criminal element hung out. You could get in trouble on Jacksboro Highway. The Skyliner was right next door to the 2222 Club. That was a big gambling casino back in the '30s or '40s. I don't know when they banned gambling, but gambling used to be legal because my uncle owned that casino. The owner ran it in the basement of the Westboro Hotel in Fort Worth.

I didn't hang out along Jacksboro Highway until I got with Cecil. He was from that side of town. Jacksboro Highway was always redneck, cowboys over in Northside. Except in the '30s and '40s, they had these nice nightclubs. The roof in the Rocket Club would go back. You could dance under the stars at night. The Skyliner, same thing, it had a push a button and the roof would go back. But most places my husband hung out was them little bars along there. There were plenty of those. A lot of the gangsters and lowlifes hung out in all the little bars."

**

"One night I got booked at a big ranch. They had an annual big to-do every year. One of the big car dealers put it out. It was a private party. They were having strip tease dancers and all the gambling stuff going on. It might have been a charity event. I don't know. I wish I could remember who owned it. I didn't know. They had a lot of money. They were upper class.

We went out there. There were me and a couple of other girls. My daddy had the gambling part. He had all the crap tables and the blackjack tables. They were set up like a casino out there in the barn and I'm like, 'Oh shit. I'm going to take my clothes off in front of my daddy.' I thought, 'Hell, I don't care.'

We're back getting dressed and all of a sudden everything got quiet. I'm like what the hell is going on? I peeped out and all of these people were up against the wall. The police were raiding it for the gambling. They confiscated all that gambling equipment. They might have taken my daddy into jail that night. I don't know. I went back and said girls, get out of here, and get your clothes on quick. Get out of the costumes.

The police talked to us, but they let us go. Anybody that had any chips or anything, they were arresting them, to fine them or whatever. I don't know. Anyway, we didn't do our show that night."

**

"One year I worked for, what did they call it, the Jewel Ball, Crystal Jewel Ball or something, at the country club over there in Arlington Heights. That was a big charity event. They hired me to strip. I was in a separate room. People had to pay extra to come in to see me dance. They had me dancing behind a screen with a silhouette because it was too risqué to actually come out like that.

I came out and danced and then I went behind the screen to take my stuff off. That was fun. That was the night I had Carter Junior back there zipping my dress up for me and helping me get in my costume, which they were the family of Fort Worth. Rich."

**

Nancy leans forward and taps on an 8-by-10 publicity photo. "I didn't feel like doing my hair that day. So that's a wig." She admires herself. "I looked like Kim Novak."

**

In Dallas, Jack Ruby struggled with his new Carousel Club. He had owned other clubs with varied levels of failure. The Carousel started as a supper club, but it wasn't working, so he decided to try it as a striptease venue. Ruby had to get girls, but he didn't want to go through booking agent Pappy Dolsen. Ruby didn't like Dolsen.

"Pappy wanted to sign girls up right away, especially new girls, to a two- or three-year contract," Nancy says. "Sherry had already told me. 'Do not sign with him, because if you do you'll have to work where he tells you to work and he'll get 20 percent. He's got control of you.' "

Sherry Lynn recommended Nancy to Ruby. He hired Nancy without even meeting her.

"He told me what he'd pay me, and then that he'd give me extra because I'd have to drive from Fort Worth to Dallas and back. And I said okay. I knew him well enough to know what to expect. He was nice to me. I did my first show, and he was pleased."

**

"After I started dancing, I rented a house. When we were getting ready to move, my grandmother moved with me. I had her, and my mother moved in eventually.

We rented another house in Fort Worth, and was living there. My grandmother said if she had all the money that she had paid out in rent over the years, she could own the finest brick house in Fort Worth. She started wanting me to buy a house.

Back then in the '60s, women couldn't buy a house, single women. It was like you just couldn't. I came home, and my grandmother said they had looked at a house. They liked it, and they wanted me to go look at it. I said, 'Okay, but I can't buy it, because I'm not married.' Your husband had to sign. It was before all this liberation.

We went and looked at this little house. It was a frame house. It wasn't fancy, but it had a nice yard. The house was a living room, dining room, kitchen, two-bedrooms, and one bath. There was a little addition on the back, like a small efficiency apartment. They had converted the garage into a mother-in-law house is what they had done.

I looked at it with the real estate guy. The lumber company, they owned it.

'I don't think I can qualify.'

'We can get around that,' he said.

He went on the note with me. He co-signed and went on the note with me. That's the way I bought the house.

At the time, we were paying $42 a month rent for a farmhouse. My new house payment was going to be $72 a month. Oh, my gosh! How am I going to afford $72?

But I had gone to work for Jack, and it worked out fine. I paid $8,200 for that house, and the payments were $72 a month. That's almost unbelievable, six percent interest."

**

Nancy says downtown Dallas looked different back when she was working there. "Downtown used to be vibrant. All the big hotels had a big showroom and a big entertainer." Several burlesque clubs operated along Commerce and Jackson streets: the Carousel Club, Montmarte Club, the Colony Club, and Theater Lounge, owned by Ruby's rivals Abe and Barney Weinstein. Across the street from the Carousel, the Adolphus Hotel had a musical comedy revue with a live orchestra called Bottoms Up. The show ran six times a week.

The Carousel Club was open seven days a week. Nancy worked from 9 pm to 2 am. The show consisted of four girls, each with her own 15-minute act. There was a band—a trio of drums, horn, and piano—that performed original music composed for each routine. Between the strip acts, the club would feature other entertainers such as a comedian, magician, or ventriloquist—maybe a puppeteer.

Tammi True's routine had a reputation for being raunchy.

"Other girls said I was the dirtiest thing they'd ever seen," she says. "I could dance, but I could do it tongue-in-cheek. I learned a long time ago that I was little and cute, and I could get away with stuff other people couldn't."

Nancy then puts aside the scrapbook. "I'd do a thing where I'd be dancing, lean over, and look through my legs," she says, standing up from the couch to demonstrate. She turns her back to me, spreads her legs, and tries to bend over. She's able to bend only at a 45-degree angle. She looks back to me and says, "Can you see the whole show?"

I laugh uncomfortably. Nancy then turns around.

"I'd do a half split."

Nancy does not attempt the half split.

"I'd fall down into it, and I'd go, 'Would you say that's stretching a good thing too far?'"

Nancy sits down.

"When I got up on that stage, I had everyone standing up on their damn feet, hollering, screaming, and hooting. You gotta work the crowd. Fifty percent of it is projection, and the other 50 percent is costuming and talent."

**

"People were actually entertained back then. The emcee would come out and do like a monologue. Tell jokes. If they played an instrument, they would play their instrument or sing. Get the crowd all warmed up, and then they would introduce the first girl. After she went off, they came back and made some kind of comments, jokes.

Harry Blackstone Jr. worked as an emcee, but

he also did magic. He was funny. He was trying to get a contract with the Playboy Club. He was talking to me about going on the road with him working Playboy Clubs as his assistant.

Walter Weston was a comedian, just a flat-out comedian. He was funny and dry. I worked with a guy named Earl Norman. He was real funny. One time we had Gene Temple. He did puppets. He had an act with puppets, but he introduced us when it was our turn."

**

"You've got to remember you're the star of the show. You've got to come out and look better, and do something better, or different than anybody else has done. You've got to project! You've got to get into it."

**

"The other performers and I used to go to the Cotton Bowl. The Cotton Bowl was at Lemmon and Inwood. It was a big place. They had pool tables and bowling. They even had bands. A lot of people would go there after hours, because they were open all night. One time, we had a little bowling league.

We had fun. It was like a little community with all of us. You had your normal rivalry, and jealousies, but basically, most of the girls were okay. They were friendly. Chris Colt had a lot of trouble, because she couldn't see. She was blind.

She had her steps counted when she was on stage—how far to go forward and how far to go over here because she's so damn blind without her glasses. She couldn't see. Somebody said one time, 'That damn Chris Colt, she's so damn stuck-up.'

'Why?' I asked.

'I walked right by her in the parking lot, the parking garage, and she didn't even speak to me.'

'Did she have her glasses on?'

'No.'

'Well, hell. She probably didn't see you.'

Nobody knew that she wore glasses."

**

"Ralph Paul was Jack's partner, and I was his girlfriend.

The club wasn't doing good. Ralph had a club and strips back in the '40s or '50s. He told Jack that he would help him out if he'd put in the strip, make it a striptease place. He was a silent partner, but he had the money to put into the club. He took a shine to me. Every year we'd go to New York for Rosh Hashanah. He was Jewish. He was a lot older than I was. He was in his sixties, I'm sure. Our relationship was weird. It wasn't a sexual type. It was more a father type. He wanted to do nice things for me.

Ralph bought me a fur coat one year and all that crap. Took me to the country, Mount Freedom, New Jersey, to Ackerman's. We went every year. We remained close even after all this happened. I wasn't a girlfriend per se. He was alone. All his family was in New York. He just wanted a companion. It was not a sexual thing. He loved to play gin rummy, so I played gin. We played a lot of gin. We'd go out to nice places for dinner. For my birthday one year, he bought me a one-carat diamond. I had it mounted with some other diamonds that I had. For Christmas, he bought the family our first color TV.

He liked the kids. He liked my mother. He liked coming over to eat. He stayed in the house a lot on the weekends, and he liked Sunday dinner. Sometimes I'd go over to his house. He lived in Arlington. He owned the Bullpen barbecue restaurant. Real good barbecue for a Jewish man. He got all that General Motors business over there. It was a real popular little restaurant. He had bought himself a house in Arlington. Sometimes I'd go over there and cook a pot roast.

There was never a problem with him as my boyfriend and Jack as my boss. When Ralph would come to the club, afterwards we would go out and eat. Jack always went with us. I spent a little more time around Jack as a result of being Ralph's friend girl. I don't know whether he was just past his sexual desire or if he was impotent. It just never was a sexual thing. I guess I was arm candy, I don't know. But if I ever got pissed off at Jack, I'd tell Ralph. Ralph would probably tell him to lay off.

Ralph started getting a little weird, like a little

bossy. Like old guys do, they get a little childish. I'd get mad at him. I'd call him, and he'd get me something pretty."

**

Ralph had been married. He had a daughter. He may have had two kids. I'm not sure. Apparently, he never talked about it. He did mention that her family didn't approve of him. There were hard feelings there. That's all I knew about that. But then when he passed away, she had been staying with him. She had come down from New York or wherever and had been staying with him in Arlington. Her name was Marilyn. I never met her. I didn't know anything about her. All those trips to New York that we made, nobody ever talked about her or anything. I don't know what that deal was.

He used to tell me, 'You need to find somebody and get married so you can have somebody to take care of you.'

'I don't think so.'

Much later, I called him and told him that I was getting married.

'Why are you doing that?'

'You always told me that I needed to find somebody and get married.'

'Yeah, but I didn't mean it. If I'd known you wanted to get married I would have married you.'

'Oh well.'

I wouldn't have married him because there

was too much difference in age. I loved him. He was sweet, and he was good. He was just a good man. If I had to live with him 24/7, that wouldn't have lasted at all.

**

Her dresses were hand-tailored by Tony Sinclair, a drag queen.

"He made costumes for another girl. I really loved her costumes. I met him when I was in Kansas City. They were having a gay convention, and I met him after work. He was being a bitch that night. I asked him about making me some costumes, but he didn't want to sew."

Nancy did not let this stop her. She began to befriend Sinclair. They worked shows together, shared hotel rooms on their travels. Then Sinclair finally relented and sewed costumes for her.

"He was right behind the curtain catching all my stuff. He made it and he wanted to take good care of it." The dresses would cost around $300, which, accounting for inflation, would be more than $2,000 today.

**

"Tony and I shared hotels rooms together. We worked together. He'd come down every year for two weeks, and I'd put him up in a motel.

My kids would go with me to the motel. He whipped them up some little bikinis one time out of some fabric. He loved the kids. He was a good-looking guy. We'd go out to eat, and the girls were always flirting with him. He'd flirt back. When we went out, he'd act real masculine.

Tony did drag in the show. He had a net bra that he had made, and he filled it with birdseed. He did a strip tease. He was drop dead gorgeous.

I went into Tulsa a week ahead of him. He was coming into work. A friend of mine had opened up a club up there. We were working in Oklahoma City together, Tony and I. They came down to see our show. I told them they really ought to get him, because he was hot!

I went in a week early. They had put pictures of him up behind the bar in the club. They also served lunch. They had all these lawyers, and people that came for lunch. I walked in there one day, and the bartender was back there.

'Tell 'em. Tell 'em that that's a boy,' he said.

'Yep, That's a boy.'

This one guy says, 'Damn! That's enough to make you want to switch.' "

**

"Jack thought I was pretty smart. I didn't drink and get drunk and do dope and do all that crazy stuff that a lot of them did. I had a good head on my shoulders and was taking care of myself."

**

As Tammi True, she was featured in the United Press International news feed for a $150,000 lawsuit against Jimmy Levens. They got into an argument. Levens turned the spotlight off on her at the Skyliner, and a customer pinched her. A lawyer friend convinced her to sue. Nancy decided to file a suit "as a lark," but it never went to trial. When Jack Ruby discovered she was in the news, he was elated. The headlines made her the headliner of his show.

"It was worth $150,000 in publicity."

**

"The headliner gets more money, usually. It also changes the order and the billing. Plus, your name is up on top of the marquee. All the other girls go on before you because you are supposed to be the big kabang at the end.

You're supposed to be the one that everybody is sitting there waiting to see. They watch these other girls just so they can see you."

**

David: Were the other girls jealous at all? Was it very competitive?

Tammi: Only with one girl. Somebody told her she was the star, and she believed it. I never cared about that. All I cared about was the job and money. I'm not going to give you her name.

David: Okay.

Tammi: She was a real bitch. The story was that she's the reason that Candy Barr went to prison. She's the one who got her to hold the weed for her. She got her sent to prison for marijuana. I don't know how many years she got. Fifteen, I think.

David: Candy Barr worked at the Colony?

Tammi: Mm hmm. This girl worked at Theater Lounge. I did work with her at Theater Lounge when I started working there. She went running through the club screaming like a banshee one night, because I had gotten more applause than she did. She was pissed. I was always careful when I was around her. I was careful about my makeup bag and case, because I didn't trust her. She was a real bitch. She was the only one that I didn't like. The rest of the girls were all fine.

**

"I learned, I observed, and I traveled.

Most of the girls in Dallas had a little act or something. Chris Colt billed herself as a girl with the 45s because she had big boobs. She did like a Western thing like Candy Barr did, a cowgirl thing. We had a girl, Diana the Huntress. She came out in a Robin Hood looking outfit with her bow and arrows. A lot of them had a little theme, something they did. But, most of them basically, did the same thing. They had different costumes.

When I started travelling, I got out, I saw girls from other areas that didn't all dance alike. I'd take a little bit here and a little bit there, and then I would choreograph. I did a lot of different stuff. When you don't travel, everybody copies from each other. You know what I mean? Without even realizing it, they're doing it.

The way I got started talking to the audience was one night some guy threw his damn hotel key on the stage. It was pretty early on, that threw me totally. This guy's throwing his damn hotel key up on the stage. I danced around and I went over there and I picked it up. My drummer, Bill Willis said, 'Tell him: if you're not there in 30 minutes, go ahead and start without me.'

I did, and the audience loved that. They laughed. I threw him the key back when I said it. I thought it, yeah, there's something to this, because audiences like to feel like they're there. A lot of the girls just came out and danced, and didn't interact. The only way I could interact is to say things. As time went on, I learned these little one-liners, and just kind of put them together, and made an act out of them. But, yeah, that's the way it started.

Comedy was a big part of my routine. I came out, and I did really sexy, dirty stuff. But I did it in a way that it was kind of tongue-in-cheek. The women did not feel threatened, because I made them laugh. They felt comfortable that I wasn't trying to seduce their husband, or boyfriend, or try to be too sexy.

These are things I learned over time. I was little, and I was cute. I was funny, and the audience, they knew that I knew that they were there, and they loved it."

**

"I'd go to work with no makeup, hair back in ponytail. I'd get back there, and I'd put on all that makeup. Pancake and all that crap, and the eyeliner, I'd put on my hair pieces and my costume.

When I walked out on that stage, I took it very seriously. The better I did, the more work I was going to get.

It wasn't that glamorous actually, because it's a job like any other job. It appears to be glamorous, but you know what I did between shows? At Theater Lounge, I had a lounge chair, a chase lounge chair that folded up. I had that in the hallway. I had a reading light stuck up on the wall and a blanket that I put over the chase lounge so I wouldn't get the marks on my body. I would lie there in between shows and read a book. I was an avid reader. I used to read all the time. That's what I did between shows most of the time. Every now and then, I'd go out.

I had these two guys that kept coming in, trying to get me to come out and sit with them. Finally a girl came back there and said, 'They really want you to come up and have a drink with them.'

'Okay. Fine.'

I threw on a little cocktail dress. I went out, stomping up there. These two guys, and I sat down. The girl came over to me, 'What will you have?'

'Give me a bottle of champagne,' I said. I didn't even like that cheap champagne.

I didn't mess around with the customers."

**

"When I went on stage, I always went on with the right attitude. Even when I didn't feel well, I would. Sometimes, depending on how responsive the audience was, I worked hard or sometimes pulled back, because I wasn't feeling well.

I believe that saying 'the show must go on.' Usually by the time I was introduced, I was fine. That part of my life was okay. Everything was good. I was making, for a girl at that time, plenty of money. My kids were healthy and happy. Everything was wonderful. I didn't have a lot of bad days.

They were harder when I was married. Didn't know what I was going to do alone with two kids, and $35 a week wasn't a lot of money. Although I was making it, I had to live with my grandmother. Once I got into burlesque, I thought 'this is okay.' I can do this and I want to be good at it and make as much money as I can. I just took to it like a duck takes to water."

**

Nancy's neighbors had no clue about her secret life. During the day, she was a PTA member who baked cookies and helped out with school carnivals.

"Our family sat down every day at 4:30 in the afternoon. We didn't watch TV and eat. We all sat down and discussed our day. Then, I would leave to go to Dallas about 7 o'clock. I didn't get home until 3 or 4 in the morning. I would go to bed and get up every day at around 10. So when my children came home, I was up and spent time with them."

Nancy stresses this point. The fame was exciting, fulfilling a lifelong desire to be in the spotlight and to be adored. But it all came back to her family. Being Tammi True allowed Nancy to buy a house for them, to support her mother and grandmother, and to do it all as a single mother.

**

David: It's hard to find true stories about Jack Ruby. I was reading somewhere that Jack Ruby was the owner of the Skyliner Bar in Fort Worth, but he wasn't.

Nancy: No.

David: But I read somewhere where someone said that he was.

Nancy: Yeah, there's lot of stuff out there that. Lot of crap out there. Right after that happened, there were a lot of people wanting to get in on the publicity. They were saying all kinds of stuff.

David: If Jack Ruby owned every bar and club that people said that he owned he would have been Donald Trump.

Nancy: At the time that all this happened, he had the Vegas Club and the Carousel Club. Now he did own the Silver Spur. He owned that once. He might have had another bar. At the time all this happened, all he had was the two clubs. There were people saying all kinds of stuff.

David: For example?

Nancy: A girl at the Colony Club, she never even worked over there. She was giving all these interviews and telling all this stuff. I'm like, "She is so full of shit." She has no idea what the hell she's talking about. Everybody knew Jack and who he was, and probably encountered him at some point, because he was everywhere. He was constantly passing out cards.

**

She's TRUE All the Way!

Formerly the star of Jack Ruby's Club Carousel, Tammi True has gone on to win added fame in night clubs across the country. This beauty who dazzled the "eyes of Texas" always leaves audiences wishing they could've seen her dance all night.

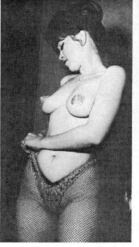

Born and raised in the Lone Star State, Tammi's family moved around Texas, until they finally decided to settle down in Dallas. It was after she graduated from high school that this lissome lass picked show business as the career to follow. She starred in the chorus line of some of the smaller niteries and in a short time became featured as the show's headliner.

"Jack Ruby had a lot of respect for me, because he knew I was independent and head strong and took care of business. All these other people during the week, they were drawing money on their salary. That's why he couldn't figure it out, because every payday, he was like 'how much money did you draw this week?'

'None.'

'Are you sure?'

'Yeah.'

He just couldn't figure that out.

I had two kids, my mother, and my grandmother. I was buying a house. My car wasn't brand new, but it wasn't shabby. I had a nice car.

There are a lot of people that, right now, they live from paycheck to paycheck. I didn't do that.

When I worked private parties, I worked high class parties. The bar association, when they had their big meetings and get-togethers, I'd work those. Charity benefits, raising money for charity. I worked for money, similar to what the girls do now in the titty bars, but not that risqué. Guys would hold money over another guy's head to get you to come over and, maybe I'd sit in their lap.

I had all my clothes on. It wasn't vulgar, nasty. I'd make money. When I got home, I'd take all the money and, whatever I got paid, I would throw it up under the bottom of our studio couch. I never touched it unless I needed some money for something. I could get under there and count it, see how much I had.

My grandmother, when I was growing up, she

always had a little bit of money kept in a sock in case of an emergency—kind of like saving her nice pajamas in case she had to go to the hospital. I was like her. I had a 'sock,' except it was a couch."

**

"My lawyer friend Charlie Baldwin defended me in court when they arrested me for being a vagrant.

I had gone to court with my income tax receipts. I had on a fur stole and a low cut dress and a hat with feathers. My reporter friends, they were all alerted that I was going to be there.

I told them I was there to prove that I made more money a year than the damn judge did. We got into court. Don Leonard was the judge. And when it came my turn, Charlie Baldwin called me to the stand. I got up there. I'm all ready to testify.

Don Leonard looked at me and he went, 'Mr. Baldwin, would you come here?'

Charlie came up there and he leaned over. I heard the judge say, 'You're not going to make a circus out of my court.' He turned around to me, he said, 'You're dismissed, young lady. All charges dropped.'

I was so mad, because I didn't get to say anything. Charlie took me to the press club for lunch afterwards and I'm griping and bitching: 'I didn't get to tell my side of the story.'

'You won!'

'Yeah,' but I said, 'I still didn't get to talk about it.' "

**

"I even brought my daughters to see a show, a very modified show. This guy I worked for, he did the luncheon shows. I told him I was going to bring them, and I was going to tone it down. He said, 'okay.'

I danced. They got to see me dance when they were about seven or eight. My oldest one was sitting at the bar ordering Shirley Temples.

The next day, she said she didn't feel like going to school. She's lying on the couch.

'What's wrong with you, honey?'

'I just don't feel good, and I am sick.'

'How do you not feel good?'

'I just don't feel good.'

In a little while she looked at me, and she said, 'Mother, these hangovers are terrible.' "

**

"I was an open book. If I've got one fault in this world, it's that I am too honest. I was always honest and open with my kids, because when I grew up it was, 'Shut up, because I said so, and I'm the boss.' Afterward, I'd get under the bed and cuss them out quietly.

I didn't want my kids to feel that way. I wanted them to be able to express themselves. I told them, 'You can say anything to me you want to say, as long as you say it the right way.' That's the way they were raised.

At holidays, I would let them have a little egg-nog with a bit of brandy in it and nutmeg. One time a friend of mine was visiting, and she had a daughter. I was going to mix us a drink, and Tracy, she's like, 'Oh, mommy. I want some. I want to drink this orange juice and vodka. I want some of that! I want some of that!'

'Okay,' I said, 'but you better go get your bath, because as soon as you drink this, you're going to be passing out. You better get ready for bed.'

She ran in there and got her bath and got her pajamas on. She came running back in there. I fixed her a glass of orange juice with a small amount of vodka, and gave it to her. My friend was listening, and she said, 'I can't believe you did that.'

'What?'

'I just can't believe you'd give her vodka.'

'That's not going to hurt her,' I said. 'When she gets a little older, some of her peers want her to get drunk and drink booze. She's going to say, Oh, I've been doing that a long time. It's not a big deal.'

Knock on wood, neither one of my kids have ever been boozers or drug addicts. I also told them, 'If you go to jail, don't call me, because I ain't getting you out.' They ain't been to jail. I've had a good relationship with my children."

**

"Tony Bennett was in Tulsa. He was signing albums at a big department store.

I was with my friend Mary. She got an album and had him sign it. He looked up at me, and he said, 'You and I have something in common.'

'We do?'

'We both wear wigs,' he said.

I had my wig on. And he wore a wig, because he was bald headed.

Mary gave him a card and told him after the concert to come on out to the club. He took the card. That night somebody called and asked if we had Italian food at the club. They said they were with Tony Bennett's party. Did we have Italian food? We said, 'Yeah.'

We didn't have Italian food. We only had steaks, but they was the best steaks you ever tasted. They were Lebanese. They did the hummus tahini, and the tabouli. The steaks were well seasoned.

In a little while, here Tony Bennett came with maybe eight or nine people. They came in and sat down. They ate and drank. I sat with him. We had our picture made together. I danced with him.

He was doing Dallas next. He did not like to fly. He was trying to get Jimmy to let me off so I could drive him to Dallas. See his concert. Go with him to see his concert, and all that. Jimmy couldn't do that, because he didn't have nobody to take my place.

I ended up taking him back to his hotel. I could have gone up there, seriously, but I didn't.

He was a nice guy, and he was stocky. When I danced with him, his arms were really muscular. He was sweet. I loved meeting him.

I always kept a cool head about the people I met. Even though they were famous and rich, I didn't let that sway me one way or another. I was always realistic about all that.

I had a movie producer who gave me a Thunderbird with a car phone. He thought he bought and paid for me with that car, and he found out right quick he didn't."

**

A priest discovered Nancy's secret after visiting her mother. Father Fisher was new to the parish, and he came to introduce himself. Nancy's mother had put some of Tammi's publicity pictures on the wall. While talking, Father Fisher kept stealing glances at the photographs. Then he had to ask, "What does your daughter do anyway?"

Her mother replied, "She's an entertainer."

Later, when Nancy was home, the priest returned to introduce himself.

"I noticed that you're an entertainer," he said.

"Yes, I am."

"What kind—"

"I'm a striptease dancer," Nancy answered directly. "I don't know whether that's a sin or not. Do you think it is, Father?"

"Are you doing it with the intention of making someone go out and do something bad?"

"No, I'm just doing it so I can get paid at the end of the week."

"Then, in that case, it's not a sin." Father Fisher paused for a moment. "But I'd be glad to come over and watch your show and let you know what I think."

Nancy declined his offer.

**

"Peter Dubois. He worked in Tulsa, and he was a friend of mine. He was on his way back from Mexico the day that Kennedy was assassinated. He was riding with some kids from New York, and they stopped at my house in Fort Worth. They were ragged and hungry. I let them spend the night there. The next day, I drove him to Dallas.

This is the day of the assassination. I drove him to Dallas because he was going to borrow some money off of a friend of his that lived in Dallas. We had maybe an hour before Kennedy got shot. We had gone down Commerce Street. The Warren Commission made a big deal about him, like he was in town as part of some conspiracy."

**

On Sunday morning, November 24, 1963, Jack Ruby drove to the Western Union to wire $25 to Little Lynn, an advance to pay her rent. He took his dog Sheba along with him. Little Lynn would've picked up the money at the club, but Jack had closed out of respect for President Kennedy who had been assassinated two days earlier.

After Jack wired the money, he noticed a crowd outside the Dallas police station where Lee Harvey Oswald was being held. Jack left his dog in the car and walked over to see what was going on.

He walked down the ramp to the basement where a group of reporters were gathered. Oswald was being transferred from the city jail to the county jail.

Jack had a gun in his right hip pocket. He always had a gun on him, since he always carried around large amounts of cash. When he saw Oswald, he pulled his gun, stepped out from the crowd, and shot him. The police wrestled Jack to the ground.

All of this took place on live television.

**

When Jack Ruby shot Lee Harvey Oswald, Tammi True's legacy would forever be tied to his club and his name. Her secret identity was revealed.

"Nobody knew what I did until Jack shot Oswald. In the paper, they put my name, my real name, and I was devastated. My neighbors were great. I had lived there long enough that they knew I wasn't a dipshit floozy. I was an ordinary, regular person. My kids took a little flack. One or two of their little friends weren't allowed to play with them. The kids would say, 'Your mom's a striiiiper,' and be ugly to them."

Nancy closes her scrapbook.

"I never participated after Jack did that. I'd never go see him. I didn't work the club. I had actually closed out to take off for Thanksgiving, and I never went back.

Ralph had kept that club open for a couple of months after all that. I guess he was trying to help out Eva, Jack's sister.

She was like Jack. I'm sure Ralph, probably, said, 'That's it. I don't want to deal with you.'

I was out of town, most of the time, working. Ralph and I had spells where we didn't talk to each other or see each other for a while. I had to take a break from him, too."

**

"I spent a while talking to the Warren Commission about Jack Ruby. They flew me in from Oklahoma City, because I was working up there. They flew me in for the day, and then I had to fly back. I had to work that night. They flew me to Dallas to the Federal building. Took my deposition. My return flight was later that evening. I had to be to work that night. I wasn't too happy about being interviewed anyway, because I wasn't going to tell them anything that they wanted to hear. I didn't have anything bad to say about Jack.

Jack was out every day hitting the pavement, talking to people, passing out cards. He had that other club for years, plus he had another club before the Vegas Club. There were a lot of people that knew Jack. They were trying to interview all these people. I think they might have interviewed my husband Chet. He knew him.

He knew him from the club business, and he went dancing at the Vegas Club a lot, as I did. I went dancing a lot, because he had that blues man that played there, Joe Johnson. They were good. They played all that blues music back in the '60s. We'd go there to dance and drink. You had to take your own bottle. You could only get a mix drink if you belonged to a private club."

**

"Did I tell you that story about Des Moines? I came out after my show, and sitting in the bar was this guy. He offered me money to come to his room after work. He kept going up on the money offer. Finally, he said, 'Everybody's got a price,' and I said, 'I didn't come to Des Moines to be a whore. I can be a whore in Fort Worth, Texas.' "

**

"I traveled all over the United States. I worked in theaters in California and Washington. I performed in a real theater on a big stage with the band in a band pit, real old time burlesque. I worked in Milwaukee, Wisconsin.

I worked Oklahoma a lot, Tulsa and Oklahoma City. I worked in Nashville, Des Moines, Kansas City, and New Jersey. I worked in Waterloo, Iowa. I didn't even know there was a town called Waterloo!"

**

"I wasn't ashamed about stripping. I felt like it was a blessing actually. I felt like God had blessed me with a way for me to take care of my children, and provide a good life for them.

What I was shooting for was for my kids to have a stable life that I didn't have—with a roof over their heads and a feeling of belonging. I had to move from this neighborhood to another neighborhood. I had a lonely life because I was an only child.

I was a lousy little kid dreaming about being Betty Grable, wearing all these costumes, dancing and singing. God did not give me a voice to sing, trust me, but I can sing with my body. I figured he gave me a drop dead gorgeous body and dancing talent, so I could survive and take care of my family."

**

"I worked for the Weinsteins, probably about 1965 or 1966. Barney called me in Omaha, and asked me if I would come in and co-star with Tempest Storm.

'But I'm not paying Pappy Dolsen any commission,' I said.

'Don't worry about that,' he said. 'I'll take care of that.'

Pappy would tell the club owners—for instance, Jimmy Voorhees at the Momar Club—that if he hired me, Pappy was going to take all the acts out. Pappy booked the other acts. He was the only agent at that time in town. Jimmy told him fine, anyway. Pappy couldn't run over Jimmy Voorhees, and he couldn't run over Barney and Abe Weinstein.

Barney paid him his commission, besides over and above my salary. I worked there until 1968.

The only other person who refused to work with Pappy was my mentor Sherry Lynn. She's the one who told me about him and Jack Cole, because he and Jack Cole were partners. She said they were going to try to get you to sign with them. They wanted exclusive contract, and they were going to sign you up for two or three years. And then you're stuck with them. You can't work anywhere without them saying it's okay. Pretty much, you have to work wherever they want you to work. She advised me not to do that."

Jack Ruby would hire girls out of town, or wherever he could get girls, who didn't work for

Pappy. Because he didn't trust Pappy, he didn't like him. I didn't have a problem with him."

**

"Pappy Dolsen looked like Colonel Sanders. He was a big guy, and he had white hair. I imagine when he was younger, he was a good looking man. He had a big nightclub on Davis over in Oakcliff, before Oakcliff went dry. It was a big. It was called Pappy's Showland. He had big name acts there. Ralph, Jack's partner, had a club across the street called the Sky Club. They were in competition. When I was a kid, I remember when we'd go to Dallas, when my grandmother finally got a car, we'd drive to visit my aunt. I remember we'd go by there. I'd look, and I'd see that it was set back in some trees. I used to always think one day I would go there, because it looked like a real fancy place."

**

"I did a little work for Pappy later on in '67, '68. Sometimes, he'd call me. Somebody was sick or they couldn't make it. He'd call me to go out the Athens Strip, one of those jukebox clubs, but it was a nice one. It wasn't on the tables. You would dance. They had a stage up behind the bar, raised. The Athens Strip was out on Greenville. That's when they had started all these neighborhood bars.

Pappy called me to go there and work, and I said okay. I'll do it. I was running a little late when I got there. The guy that owned the place was mad.

When I got there, he said, 'You're late!'

I was carrying all that stuff in, and I said 'I don't need this job. I will leave.'

'No, no just get ready, just go ahead and get ready.'

I ended up going on, in the headliner's spot, because I was late. I don't remember why I was late—usually I was never late—probably because I didn't care about working there.

I went out there and did my show. Then I came back to the dressing room,

'You just keep going last for the rest of the night,' he said.

He and I had become friends. He found out real quick that he couldn't act like that with me, because I was pretty damn independent."

**

The Texas Court of Appeals overturned Jack Ruby's death sentence and was scheduled to grant him another trial. However, on January 3, 1967, Jack died of a pulmonary embolism related to lung cancer.

"Ralph went to the funeral, but he didn't go inside the synagogue. He stood out across the street from it. He didn't want to because of media publicity, but he did want to go out of respect. He went but he didn't go in. He just stood across the street while they were having the service. I don't know whether he went to the cemetery or not. Jewish faith, they want to bury them within 24 hours.

Jack was pretty proud about his faith. He wasn't kosher. He tried to be kosher. He was close. He ate a lot of lamb. I don't recall ever seeing him eat any bacon or pork. He went to synagogue. He had a rabbi and he attended synagogue regular. He wasn't a heathen."

**

Nancy found work at Weinstein's club, Theater Lounge. She would sometimes fill in at the Colony Club, and would run back and forth between the clubs to perform, changing in between. Nancy also found steady work in Oklahoma. But burlesque entertainment waned in the '60s and '70s. By the early '80s, none of these Dallas clubs would survive. The once vibrant downtown Dallas would be reduced to parking garages and office buildings.

Nancy noticed the downward trend. The girls started dancing to "canned music," and the band was no longer used. It was more economical for club owners. In exchange, the clubs lost a bit of their glamour and class. The strip clubs lost the variety show aspect as well. No more comedians, magicians, or ventriloquists. New bars opened along Greenville Avenue, near the Granada Thea-

ter, featuring smaller stages and catering to a
lunchtime crowd. Where once women crafted rou-
tines, now they just danced naked. The expedience
of these new clubs sidestepped the bawdy fun of
burlesque, and it became seedier as a result. Nancy
withdrew back into civilian life. She remarried.

"At the age of 30, I hung up my G-string."

**

"My next door neighbor had ordered some
manure for his flowerbed and yard. He came over,
and said, 'Nancy, I've got some of this manure
left. Do you want some for your flowerbeds?' I
said, 'Yeah.' He got the wheelbarrow and brought
me some, and we were putting it out.

I stood up. I'm sweating and cow shit all over
me, and I'm like, 'If my fans could only see me
now.' He laughed, and he said, 'You know what?
If your fans could see you now, they'd probably
even like you more,' because I was a real person."

**

"I retired from burlesque when I married Ben.
We got married December 1968. I had also gone
to school. I knew how to do electrolysis. I opened
up my own little place in a health club and did
electrolysis, facials, and the false eyelashes. I had
some wealthy customers from North Dallas. I had
one gal that liked to slum. She would come make
her appointment, and she would come in early and

say, "Let's go to the Athens Strip!" Her name was Gerri. I forget what her last name was. I'd take her over there and have a drink and watch the girls dance. We had a lot of fun.

My mother got sick in 1971. She had cancer. She was dying. She was terminal when we found out. I stayed with her at the hospital. As an only child, she didn't have anybody to help except her sister, my aunt. We both stayed at night. One of us would go home during the day every other day. I had to give my business up, close it down.

After my mother passed away, Gerri called and I would take my equipment and go to her house. Her pool house was bigger than my house that I lived in at the farm.

My husband and I opened a clothing store in downtown McKinney. The name of it was The Wearhouse. We sold discount jeans.

I worked for the Credit Bureau, the McKinney Retail Merchants Association. They decided to close my office. I hung around my store for about a year. I kept saying I didn't like being with my husband 24/7. I kept saying, 'I'm gonna go find me a real job!'

My aunt's son's wife worked for a place in Dallas called Southwestern States Bankcard Association, SSBA for short. She said, 'Go down there. Susan says they're always hiring, always need people down there.'

I kept fiddling around and not doing it. She would say, 'Have you been down there yet?'

'No.'

'I told you, you need to go.'

Finally one day I thought, 'Hell, I'm just going to go down there and put in an application just to get her off my ass.'

I was going to town to have lunch with a friend of mine that worked at Texas Instruments. I stopped in there and I filled out an application. They interviewed me. Somebody talked to me in human resources. Fine, got that over with.

By the time I got home they were on the phone calling me, wanting me to come back. I didn't know when I could come back. I got the job. I wasn't looking for a job, but I got a job.

I went to work for them, and I stayed with them for 15 years. That's banking and credit card banking business. That's where I retired from."

**

"From 1960 to 1968, my life was absolutely wonderful. And it wasn't bad after that. I married Ben and things were fine. We bought the place in the country, had a garden. We started raising horses, and doing all these farm things. That was new and different for me because I was raised in town. That was fine.

Then he and I got cross-ways. I've always been the type that I'm not going to let anybody disrespect me or insult my intelligence or abuse me or try to run over me. Once I got rid of Cecil Powell, I decided that is it. I'm not taking any bull from anybody ever again. He'd lie, 'Oh, I'm going to do better blah, blah.' I'd go back to him and it'd be the same thing.

I decided when I divorced him that I was never going to be in that situation again because if they disrespected me or cheated on me, that was it."

**

"Tracy dated this boy in high school that was a working at a horse breeding ranch. He worked in the stables there. He had a Corvette. He let her drive his Corvette, and she was pulling up in the drive way in that Corvette like 'hee-hee-hee!'

We were raising horses too. We knew all of those people around there that raised horses.

I never worried about Tracy. One night, this boy came and picked her up. He walked to the back door. I never said to him, 'You have to be back at a certain time.' I always said, 'What time are you going to be home?' They knew it had to be reasonable. They couldn't tell me three or four o'clock in the morning, but I always let them set their time. They'd be more likely to be back if they set the time than me demanding a time.

He turned around to me and said 'Oh, don't worry about her. I'll take real good care of her.'

'Oh, I'm not worried about her,' I said. 'I'm more worried about you.'

She doesn't take any bullshit. Those boys want to try to get in her pants, and she won't go out with them anymore. She wasn't about to do that. I didn't have to worry about her. Not to say she didn't like boys, but her sister had gotten pregnant, and she wasn't going there."

**

"My second husband I were married December 28th, 1968. His name was Ben Stailey. I think we separated in `78, and I stayed gone a year. He kept begging me and begging me, and I went back. I didn't drop the divorce, though. I had already filed divorce. I left him again, and that's when I ran into Chet.

Chet was bad about when we'd go out, and someone would say something about me. He'd say, 'Oh, she's married. She's got a husband.'

My lawyer had called me and said, 'We are either going to have to drop this thing or go ahead and go through with it.'

'Just go through with it,' I said.

He wasn't even there. They didn't contact him or anything. He didn't know that he was divorced from me until I told him."

**

"I didn't marry Ben because I had to marry Ben. I did it because I wanted to. Ben had his bank account, I had my own personal bank account, and we had a joint bank account. I didn't need him at all. I still owned my house in Fort Worth. I was totally independent, even though I got married.

'What you make will be our fun money,' he said. 'I'll pay all the bills and all that, and we'll do things and have fun with your money.'

'Fine.'

That was our deal and I bought all the groceries and all that, but he always paid all the bills and the insurance payments and all that."

**

"I like being in Texas. It's my home. I grew up in Fort Worth, and I thought I'd live out my whole life in Fort Worth. It was a lot different for me when I moved to McKinney and married Ben. That was a total new life.

Our place was about two and a half miles east of Allen. There was hardly anything in Allen. There was one grocery store. Once you went through Allen, you better have bread, milk, anything you needed because if you didn't, then you had to drive all the way back to Allen or McKinney to get it.

I adapted to country life. I became a horse breeder. I started a big garden and learned to can. I did all the normal things that married couples would do. People couldn't believe I did that, that knew me from when I was dancing. They were like 'You're living up on that farm?'

'Yeah, I'm wading in horse shit.'

They couldn't imagine me living on a farm raising vegetables and canning. A lot of people, when you're working with them, they don't know, what kind of a person you are inside. It's what they see at work. Everybody thinks what I did, that show business is glamorous. It's not.

I mean it's work. It's lonely traveling on the road being away from family and friends. I was lucky enough that every place I ever worked, I managed to make some friends. That was nice, to have people to be friends with."

**

"I worked in north Dallas. After work, I'd go home. I would change clothes. I would go out and pick vegetables. We had two refrigerators. I had one in the garage. I had two deep freezers, and I would pick all my vegetables. I would put them in bags and set them in that refrigerator. The next night when I went home, I would start getting them ready to can or freeze. I'd fill the freezer.

In the wintertime, we didn't have to buy a lot of vegetables. Ben would go to the auction and buy those little bull calves, cheap, like $10 or $15. We'd bring those home, and he'd fatten them up and take them to the feeding lot and have them cut up into meat.

He fed the horses when he got home and made sure they had water. I helped him with the breeding, and holding the mare. Hell, I had to wear rubber boots because if it was wet and muddy out there in the horse pens, I had to have on my rubber boots. I had been raised in the city.

I didn't know anything about living in the country, but I liked it.

I made pickles. I made good pickles. I make pickled squash. I was kind of famous for that. I made hot sauce. Some of those batches were kind of hard, because your eyes would be burning. If you cut up jalapenos, you happened to forget and touch yourself, then you were on fire.

I had okra. I had radishes. I had squash. I had everything. I planted everything except corn. In the first year, we planted corn but the horses got out. They went to the corn and messed it up. It didn't make enough really. We had a guy out toward Frisco who had cornfields. He would call us whenever the corn was ready to pick. Ben and I would get up early that morning. We'd go out through the cornfields, and we would pick corn. We'd fill up the bed of the pickup with it.

It wasn't anything for us to buy 50 dozen ears of corn. It's like three or four cents an ear, if we picked it. We'd take it home, and I'd have the kids all out, and his family. We'd have a 4th of July party, because that's when corn is usually ready."

**

"Ben and I started having problems. He started not showing up. I figured he's doing something he's not supposed to be doing. He wasn't going to admit that.

In 1978, I filed for divorce. He was not taking

care of the store like he should. We had hired a young girl, a student to come afternoons and work. When she'd get there, he would take off and go to Dallas, titty bars, or whatever the hell he was doing.

The store was going downhill. I left him, and I filed for divorce.

I liquidated the business. I sold the building, paid off all the debts. Ben didn't argue about anything because he knew he had done the wrong thing.

When I filed for divorce, he said he didn't see any point in getting a lawyer and wasting money.

'Fine with me,' I said. 'You can use mine.'

We used the same lawyer. He just went down to her office. He signed everything.

The only thing he got in the divorce was his old Cadillac and some tools. Everything else was mine.

I did agree to let him live at the house as long as he wanted. As long as he made the mortgage payment and paid the insurance, he could live there. I wasn't ready to sell it. I knew that someday it was going to be worth quite a bit of money."

**

"What went wrong was probably that 40-year itch that men get. They've been married a while, and they get to feeling neglected. It's kind of like women going through menopause. I call it the

40-year itch.

Marriage is hard. The honeymoon ends, and it's real life. You're dealing with all kinds of things during the day. You're tired at night. You don't have time to go stroke your partner every day.

Life is hard, especially when you've got children. I think he just kind of got to that point. He didn't feel appreciated, or he didn't feel like our romance was hot enough.

He liked going out and hanging out. He's a good-looking guy. He didn't have any problems. He didn't have to work hard for the girls to like him. They were stroking him and laughing and all that crap that I did whenever I worked. Being nice to the customer. He was loving it.

I didn't care enough to follow him around and try to catch him. I didn't care. I had already done that with my first husband, and I wasn't going to do it with him.

When he started not coming home at night, and being late every night, I didn't like being out there in the country by myself at night. It was dark, and I was not comfortable being out there. That was the main thing that I hated.

One night, I got a call about two in the morning. Someone called to tell me the store had been broken into. The window had been broken out. Ben was their contact, but he wasn't there. I told them he's not here. He's supposed to be at the store.

He finally came in.

'Where have you been?'

'I was at the store. I had to do inventory.'

'Really? Were you there whenever they broke the plate glass window out and came in and robbed it?'

'What?'

'The store's been broken into and robbed. The security people or police or whoever it was, they called. They were wanting to know where you are so they can fix it or board it up.'

He called them, then he took off. That was it for me. I got me some boxes and brought them home and put them in the spare bedroom.

He was getting ready to go to work, got ready, and went out the door to get in the car. I went in there and got my boxes and had them all spread out in the living room and the bedroom. He came back. He forgot something in the house. He came back. He stepped in the door

'What are you doing?'

I looked at him and I said, 'I'm moving. I'm leaving.'

'I don't know why you're doing this.'

'Ben, I believe you. I am totally convinced that you do not know why I'm leaving you so don't even go there. I'm leaving and that's it.'

He turned around and left to go to work.

He signed the divorce papers, then he's calling me, begging me, pleading with me all the time.

'Please come back.'

I know he loved me, but men are a different animal. They can love their wife and their family and still go screw around. That is a normal thing.

They do that. I was never worried about him leaving me for somebody else.

Three things I never shared with my friends: my toothbrush, my douche bag, and my husband. I have strong feelings about being married and making a commitment, taking vows. You got a problem; you need to be able to sit down with your partner and talk about it, work it out.

I've had guys coming up trying to put the make on me and, 'Oh yeah, I'm married but my wife and I have an arrangement. I'm not happy in my marriage.'

'If you're not happy then why don't you leave.'

'I'd do that, but I have kids.'

'Why make your kids miserable?'

You know men are just weird, and I have studied men all my life."

**

"Ben never remarried or anything. I'd go up there every now and then and visit. He'd be excited about it every time I'd call him and tell him I was going to come up. A lot of times, I'd spend a day or two up there. He'd tell me, 'I went to the store and bought you some Blue Bell ice cream. It's in the freezer.' He always made sure I had some Blue Bell ice cream, because he knew I liked it.

We stayed friends. I used to tell people I don't want to have sex with you, and you don't want to have sex with me, because I'll put something on you that water won't wash off and that I'll never get rid of. I could never seem to get rid of these guys."

**

"I've always been able to go with the flow. Life changes. People change. I never was one to say 'Why me?' I always figured 'Why not me?'

I just stop and think okay, this is not working, and I need to figure out where I'm going to go from here. I've pretty much always had tunnel vision when it comes to my life.

I don't have many problems with change. I go with the flow. If I become unhappy with whatever is going on, then I do something different. Some people are in a rut and they just can't get out of it.

I don't hold grudges. If somebody does something to me bad, hurt me or make me feel bad, I can forget that and put it behind me.

I don't forgive them. I never forgive them, but I can forget it and move on. Does that make sense?

I could've grown up to say 'if it hadn't been for my mother or my daddy abandoning me, I wouldn't be like this.'

That's bullshit. That made me. The things that went on in my life at an early age made me want to do better than that. I don't take that for an excuse.

I've always told my kids, don't blame somebody else for what you've done. If you get caught doing the crime, then you're going to do the time. They understand that, my two kids do. That's just the way, that's life. If you're going to do something you shouldn't be doing and if somebody catches you doing it, well, it's 'okay, I did it.' Those are lessons that I learned, and I've always tried to treat people the way I wanted to be treated.

You know, I've lived pretty much by the Ten Commandments, mostly, and the Golden Rule. I have a real knack for bringing people in and God blessed me with something, that people like me. Most people, they just, they like me. And that's good. That's the way I want it.

I don't bullshit around with people. I don't get friendly and then talk about them. If I've got anything to say about anybody, I unload on them.

My good friends, which I've had some for over 50 years, they don't get mad or huffy-puffy. When I tell them something, that's just what I feel."

**

"I belonged to a dance club. They would meet on Tuesday or Wednesday nights. It was a Wednesday night. I was sitting there and this nice looking, tall, grey headed man walked up and he said, 'Don't I know you from somewhere?'

'You need a lot of help,' I said. 'Sit down and

shut up.'

He did. He sat down.

Sure enough, he did know me.

When I was 14 years old, my boyfriend Chuck was in the Air Force, and that's when I first met Chet, because he was in the Air Force with Chuck. He was nine years older. I would've been jailbait for him anyway.

He mentioned Chuck and he said, 'You're that Nancy Bolen, right?'

Our lives just crisscrossed. He knew Jack. He knew everybody. I used to stay with a girl I worked with. Sometimes, I would spend the night so I didn't have that long drive to Fort Worth. He was dating her at the time.

Chet asked me out on a date, and that was the beginning of our relationship.

We were together for 29 years. He was a great guy. Everybody loved Chet."

**

"My third marriage was to Chet Myers. He was a part of the night-life in Dallas. He was a real important part. He worked at the Statler Hilton downtown when they built that. He went to work there. He worked at the Cabana when they opened it, and that was people from Caesar's Palace, and Doris Day was connected someway in the financial part. He ran Nero's Nook. They had all those goddesses. The girls who were supposed to be goddesses like they did at Caesar's Palace, and it was a real hotspot; big entertainment there. That was where they had the big shows.

He used to brag about going to college. I said, 'what the hell good did it do you? You've been a damn glorified waiter all your life, is all you've been.'

We were married April 29th, 1990. We lived together for a few years before we got married. He had a house. He had just been divorced for a couple of years when we ran into each other. I wasn't looking for a husband, I'll tell you, but we clicked. We knew all the same people, and our lives had just been like this ever since I was 14. We were in the same circles. We had a perfect relationship. Everybody envied our relationship."

**

"When Chet and I got married, I asked him about what we wanted to do about my bank account, because that was my way to have my own money.

'Better leave it like it was,' he said.

He didn't have a separate account. He did when we first got together, because he was still working.

When he retired, and we moved to the lake. We had a joint account, but I still had my checking and my savings. I kept it all. I didn't throw it all in the pot.

I've never been dependent on anybody except Cecil. That was another part of the lesson I learned. I thought that I was getting married and he was going to take care of me and the kids. That didn't happen. I had to wake up.

I learned pretty quickly that you don't grow up and get married and live happily ever after. Which I kind of thought you did in a normal family. That isn't the way it works.   Anyway, Cecil even made me tougher. I tell my kids, even a roommate, you go to move in and get an apartment with a roommate, make sure that if that roommate flakes out on you that you can handle the rent. Because you don't ever know what people are going to do. There are a lot of flakes.

Even if they got married, be sure that they can pay what they need to pay."

**

"Chet went to college. He went to Austin College. He was going to be a Presbyterian minister. Everybody gets a big kick out of that, because he was wilder than a March hare and so much fun. He understood the Catholic religion. He studied religions. A friend of ours, Gene, made some kind of remark about Catholicism. I don't get upset; I don't care. I just figure they're ignorant. We were in Spain and he made some kind of remark. My thing was going to the Vatican when we went over there, and that was pretty exciting for me. The churches always were a big thing for me.

Chet jumped on him. He's telling him he didn't know what in the hell he was talking about.

He started explaining the Catholics. Gene is sitting there going, 'Okay.' It upset him when anybody said anything. He knew his religion. Plus he was an avid reader. All those trips we took, he knew all the history about all this stuff. Tell you all about it."

**

"Chet and I were in Morocco. These people were trying to get me to buy stuff.

'I don't have any money,' I said. 'No money."

'Oh, come on.'

'I don't have any money,' I said, 'That's my wallet back there.'

One boy said, 'That's your husband?'

'Yeah.'

'Oh, he's too big for you.'

We've been everywhere. We've gone over to Europe two or three different times. We did Portugal, and came all down that side. We went across into Morocco. We went all around.

The architecture is wonderful. The people, they still buy fresh everyday at market. The guide said the only thing they have to use a refrigerator for is cold drinks, because they don't eat leftovers. They go to the market every day. I loved it over there.

We came back across, and we went on a ship. We came by Gibraltar, came into Spain, Costa de Sol.

We were on a bus. The guide says, 'Over here

we have the beach. The nude beach.' When he said that all the guys jumped up and ran over to that side of the bus to look at it, and I'm like, 'God, y'all are going to tip the bus over.'

We did a lot. We went to Paris and Rome. We went to Rome twice. We did all of Italy. We loved Italy. We loved Spain. We were in Madrid a couple times, and Toledo, and Barcelona. One year, we did Asia.

Both of us had four weeks of vacation. We would take the three weeks, and we would plan a trip in Europe or Asia. One week, every year, we went to Mexico and spent a week in Mexico.

**

"We played a lot of golf. I finally learned. When we first started going, I didn't play golf. I rode with him in the cart, and all these nice, beautiful golf courses. Finally, I decided I should play golf. He set me up with some lessons at the country club with one of his assistant pros. I had a girlfriend who worked at Ben Hogan over in Fort Worth. I went over there and bought me a set of golf clubs. That was good.

I was ticked off. I was 50 years old, and I should have learned when I was 20, because I was a good golfer. I didn't even know I was good. But the first lesson, I was hitting the ball over 200 yards.

I was up there one day on the driving range practicing. This man came over, and Chet was with me.

'You hit the ball better than any of the ladies on the ladies golf team,' he said.

'I do?' I'd only had a couple lessons.

'You hit that ball far.'

I got in the company tournament. I was so nervous that morning. I thought I was going to throw up. I went out and played that day. I won all of the ladies prizes. Our team came in third in the overall tournament. I couldn't believe it. After that, we played about everywhere we went, just about.

The secret is to keep your head down when you're getting ready to hit the ball. You got to keep that head down and follow through.

I thought, why would people want to go out and knock a little ball around? It's peaceful. It's nice to be out. I walked the course a lot. I had a cart that I could put my clubs on and pull. It's quite, and peaceful. The birds are chirping. Then you see a squirrel running around. I wasn't that serious. I joined the ladies golf club down there at the Cedar Creek Country Club. We had our own cart.

'Anybody that's got a cart,' they said, 'let somebody ride with you who doesn't have a cart.'

'Yeah, but if they don't smoke, drink, or cuss, they don't want to ride with me.' "

**

"Chet and Cecil were big buddies. When I had sold the farm and I had promised the kids, all the grandkids, that I would take them to Disney World. I sold it, so we were all going down there. Chet didn't want to go.

'Dawn wants her daddy to go,' I said. 'She's going to pay his way.'

He didn't have a problem with that. I told the travel agent. She was booking rooms.

'I don't want to have to share a room with my ex-husband,' I said.

'What about your husband now?'

'Oh, he's not going and he doesn't care.'

People couldn't understand. I called Cecil, referred to him as Chet's ex-husband in-law. Everybody's saying, 'You've got the best of both worlds. You've got Chet and you've got Cecil. When one of them can't do something, the other one can.'

They would tell each other jokes and they got along great. Chet had no problem with me going to Florida for a week with him."

**

David: Can you tell me about retirement? When you finally—

Nancy: It sucks. You know how you sit around all day and think, "If I didn't have to work, ooh, I could do something!" Well guess what? In about a month or so, you got it all done.

**

"My husband and I retired and built a house down at Cedar Creek Lake, right on the water. I was busy at first because we were selling our home in Las Colinas, building that house, and moving a trailer across the street all at the same time.

Once we got settled, I'd go out there on my deck, and sit and look at the lake and say, 'Well, another shitty day in paradise.'

It was so boring, oh god, in Gun Barrel City, where we lived. The name was kind of fun. I'd call somebody in New York or somewhere that needed my address and I'd say, 'Gun Barrel City, Texas!'

I'd always get a laugh out of them. I'd say, 'And our motto is, we shoot straight!'

We lived down there for 13 years. Then my husband got sick. That's when I decided we should move closer to my kids. He didn't want to move, but it got to the point where he could not do anything."

**

" 'We should have gotten together when we were younger,' I once said to Chet.

He laughed and looked at me.

'No,' he said. 'You wouldn't have liked me back then, because I was a real asshole.'

Then, not too long before he died, I said, 'Do you remember when you told me that you were a real asshole when you were younger? I've got news for you. You're still an asshole.' "

**

"Chet passed away June 13th, 2009 right after my birthday. In `97, we found out that he had a tumor in his bladder, and it was cancer. They removed tumors out of his bladder three or four times, and finally they decided they just were going to have to take his bladder. He had been taking chemo right before he died, and he had made the decision to stop his chemo on Wednesday. We had gone to his urologist. He told him that he was not going to take anymore chemo, and the urologist agreed with him because he was so sick. It made him really sick.

That was Wednesday, and on Saturday, I had to call an ambulance. I just thought he was having an anxiety attack, actually, and I took him to the hospital. They decided to keep him overnight. I told the doctor. I said, 'Now, you better make sure you are going to keep him overnight, because don't call me at 2:00 or 3:00 in the morning wanting me to come get him, because I am not coming to get him.'

'Yeah,' Chet said. 'She's been trying to give me away to somebody.'

I turned around, and said, 'I'll pay child support to any of you all that want him.'

Everybody laughed, and he laughed. That's the kind of relationship we had. That was the last words I spoke to him. I said, 'Goodbye. I'll see you tomorrow.' They called me about 9:00 and told me that he was Code Blue."

**

"After Chet passed away, I settled in. I wasn't sure I'd like living by myself, because I never lived by myself before. But guess what, I loved it. I would get up, and do what I wanted to, work my puzzles, and drink my coffee.

Actually, I'm thinking about moving and not letting anybody know where the hell I live."

**

"Right after that, an article came out in the Dallas Morning News that I was dead. Nope. I don't think so.

That's what started this whole thing, the return of Tammi True.

Chet would be loving it if he was here. Oh god. He just loved telling people. All the doctors and everybody, he'd tell them, 'This is Tammi True. You don't know who Tammi True is? She worked for Jack Ruby.'

These doctors would look at me. It's hard to imagine."

**

Burlesque has returned to Dallas. It's a new

attempt at restoring theatrics and glamour to the fine art of removing clothing to music. Viva Dallas Burlesque produces sold-out shows at the Lakewood Theater every month. They feature the biggest-name burlesque dancers from all over Texas. Viva Dallas produced a Cirque du Soleil-inspired show with aerial acrobatics, juggling, and a snake charmer. Yes. Midair striptease. Troupes such as the Lollie Bombs introduce new burlesque stars to a new audience. According to Shoshana Portnoy, a photographer and the editor of Pin Curl Magazine, "It's so much more. A lot of people go for the sexuality and they go for the glamour, of course, but there's comedy. It's an entire theatrical production. Once you go, you'll know how different it is."

Dallas is the premier burlesque city in the South. The reputation of Dallas being plastic is actually well suited for burlesque, where everything is supposed to be glitzy, playful, high-flying, and artificial. Dallas is a city that likes to be entertained. Not that burlesque thrives in Dallas, but Dallas, it seems, thrives in burlesque.

The mystique of Jack Ruby, Tammi True, and the Carousel Club has fueled the imaginations of new performers.

I met one burlesque dancer, Pixie O'Kneel, who says, "I really respect the ladies from back in the day. They worked their asses off and were truly artists. Not that burlesque performers today don't work their asses off and are not artists, I just think it was harder for them than it is for us because of the way society of that time perceived women and people who were onstage."

Last year, the Ruby Revue Burlesque Show invited Nancy to appear at the House of Blues for its show. They sent a limo for her.

Angi B Lovely met Tammi True that night.

"She came backstage and told us she'd be watching to see if we were doing it right," Angi says. "Made me nervous as hell. She went onstage later that night and absolutely blew me away. I love watching the legends. There is so much to learn."

Though Nancy enjoyed herself, she criticizes the lack of live music and a comedian. "I told them you need to do it the right way. It wasn't just girls—boom, boom, boom."

**

David: The other performers praise you and make you their matron saint of Dallas Burlesque.

Nancy: Yeah, the girls have always been good to me. They treat me really, really good like I'm precious cargo.

David: They do. That was what was cool to see all these other performers coming up to you asking for your autograph. On some level, your interaction with them validates the work that they're trying to do.

Nancy: I'm sure it does. They call themselves the Ruby Review. I validate them. You're right.

David: It makes them feel like they're part of this longer tradition. It's sweet.

Nancy: It was to their benefit for me to perform with them. The first time they wanted me to come to the House of Blues. They wanted to introduce me. I did a little bit, and they were just blown away. The next time it was, "Do you think you could do a little bit this time, a little act?" I said, "Like what?" I said, "About what I did last time?" "Oh yeah, that would be great." I'm like, "That wasn't anything. I wish I could do what I used to."

**

Teddy's Room, a burlesque-themed nightclub, opened in Dallas. It features a brief show, with a single dancer, twice during the night. I went one evening by myself. I stood in the corner with my rum and Coke. Clusters of woo-girls, each wearing the same uniform black dress, crammed into the bar. I counted five bachelorette parties. It was a stylish place. The room pulsed with pop songs.

Close to midnight, the music stopped. Everyone dancing looked mildly irritated. A three-piece band on the narrow stage behind the bar broke into a swanky version of Nirvana's "Smells Like Teen Spirit." Then a twiggy woman in a black sequined dress appeared from the edge of the bar.

She rocked her hips from side to side, leaned against the back wall, and gave a high kick. In a move that reminded me of Nancy, she spread her legs and bent over, looking at the audience from between her thighs. The audience couldn't quite figure out how to respond. A piece of clothing came off and then another. The crowd grew increasingly excited and confused. When the final piece came off, revealing a sheer bra with pasties underneath, the audience applauded. The music resumed and so did they.

The days of Tammi True may have returned, but it was for a moment, and it was fleeting.

**

At Nancy's house, after putting away the plastic bin, she stands in front of me, her audience. She holds her arms up, as though waiting for the music to start, turning her head to the side.

"When I walked out, I was a star," she says. "I was going to do a good show and wow them. I took it very seriously." Her arms fall to her sides. She looks at me and shrugs.

"And when I was through, I was just plain old me."

**

"I've had a pretty interesting life. I must admit. It's been pretty remarkable.

Just coming from nothing, nowhere, no hope, and doing something with my life, turning my life around—if I can do it, anybody can do it. That's what I tell these kids. You've got to do it. Life doesn't happen. You have to make it happen.

My daughters, especially Dawn, she's been begging me for years to write it all down. They even bought me that tape recorder, I don't know, seven or eight years ago, because I've been telling her stories about this and that.

'Mother, you need to write a book,' she said.

'Well, I can't. I'm not a writer.'

'You need to put it on tape. We can get somebody else to write it.'

They had a great childhood and a weird childhood. At the time, they wanted June Cleaver for a mother, but they had a lot of fun having Nancy Powell/Tammi True for a mother.

Anyway, after they got grown, and I've been telling them these little tidbits, and then their daddy fills them in on a few things. I'm like, 'My god. Why did you tell that?' They're thrilled about it. The great grandkids are excited. They're excited that their great grandmother was a stripper."

**

Epilogue

Ginger Valentine said she would put us on the list. I had emailed her a few weeks earlier and explained that I was writing a book about Tammi True. My wife and I wanted to attend the Dallas Burlesque Festival to see Tammi perform.

The person in the ticket booth looked around to find "the list" or any tickets that might have been set aside. Nothing. She looked apologetic.

"I'm sorry. Hold on, just another minute," as she checked every corner of her booth.

The line behind us was getting impatient. I was *that guy* holding up everything.

I certainly looked like someone who would be on this mythical list. I was wearing the sloppy business casual uniform of a writer—with my corduroy sports coat, plaid shirt, jeans, and Converse. I had my steno notepad and voice recorder. I looked like a writer working on a book, which I was. So, I did something to expedite the process.

I lied.

"I'm working with D Magazine on a feature about burlesque."

All of this was factual, except the verb tense. D Magazine published that story months ago.

After the magazine feature came out, I realized there was too much to Tammi True's life—too many scandalous tidbits, too many odd anecdotes. I enjoyed talking with Nancy, and Nancy's life felt like a book. She was more than Jack Ruby. I saw a story about a girl whose mother wrecked her life on alcohol and men. Nancy could've gone the same route with Cecil, but she didn't. She could've turned into another lost cause in the juvenile justice system, but she didn't. She could've been another poor single mother depending on the kindness of her extended family. Instead, she found a way to buy a house and support her family—through burlesque. Anyone can strip. She was an entertainer, a comedian, and a star. And she had a hell of a good time. She could've given up once she was exposed, but she didn't. She kept going. And years later, she found true love, yes, her soul mate in Chet Myers. They shared many happy years together, and then he died. She could've hidden away in her grief, but she didn't. Nancy discovered that she actually enjoyed living by herself (an odd dramatic climax, but appropriate). Ultimately, the best way she could honor her late husband was to be happy. She stepped into the spotlight – and brought Tammi True back to life.

Tammi True was the alter ego, the fearless and opportunistic other self. Tammi was in charge and independent. She didn't give a damn. And she was very, very cool. Nancy wasn't the victim of a depraved society that forces poor beautiful women to work at strip clubs. In this case, Nancy was a natural exhibitionist and performer who found her voice through burlesque. Nancy was having fun on that stage, and she was nobody's victim.

Soon after the release of the magazine feature, Katie Dunn at AMS Pictures contacted me. She wanted to make a movie on Nancy's life. In particular, the movie would cover her experiences in Dallas during the '60s and her interactions with Jack Ruby. Katie and I had lunch at the Café Brazil in Deep Ellum. We talked for an hour about Nancy and Dallas burlesque. And so, fifty years after Nancy's friend would shoot Lee Harvey Oswald on live television, Nancy would have a movie about her life and a book. That book would become this book.

I took the same approach as AMS Pictures. We were both confronted with the problem of how to tell her story, but the solution was obvious. Let Nancy speak, and get out of the way.

The girl in the ticket booth gave up.

"Just go inside. It'll be fine."

Inside the House of Blues, I found Nancy and Dawn. They were standing against the wall, away from the stage and the crowd. We talked for a bit. I asked Nancy about her costume for tonight. She said, "I brought it here in a matchbox. It's two band-aids and a cork."

She winked and then excused herself to go have a smoke.

Dawn and I talked about the book. She wanted a status report. I told Dawn how all the events in Nancy's life keep blurring together. It's hard enough to keep track of her three husbands.

"She had four husbands," Dawn said.

"The roller derby guy. He doesn't count."

"No, there was another one."

"Another one?"

And this is how it is with Nancy. You think you have the whole story, and you find out about another husband, or that she tried to shoot and kill Cecil, or that Tony Bennett once propositioned her, or that Jack Ruby and her lived in the same apartment building, or some other piece of her life that caused you to wonder what else was missing. Like a burlesque routine, Nancy coyly teased out these details over time for greater effect.

When Nancy returned, some burlesque performers surrounded her. They were fans. She signed autographs and hugged them.

The other acts took the stage. They were an entertaining showcase of odd talents and personalities. The lineup included Darlinda Just Darlinda, Grace Gotham, Coco Lectric, Lula Hoop Garou, Jeez Louise, Honey Cocoa, Melissa Meaow, Black Mariah, Angi B Lovely, Angela Ryan, and Ginger Valentine. Tammi True's routine was buried in the second act.

"Are you ready for an extra special treat?"
The emcee shouted into the perfectly adequate
microphone. She paced casually, placing awkward
emphasis on every second or third word.

"Up next is a rare treat for this stage, she's a
living legend of the original Dallas burlesque scene
of the 1960s. She performed all over the country
and was a headliner locally at Jack Ruby's Carousel
Club and also performed at the Skyliner, Weinstein's Theater Lounge and the Colony Club. Are
you ready to see how the originals bumped and
grind? Please welcome our own Dallas legend,
Tammi True!"

Was I ready? Modern burlesque producers
talk about how they want to celebrate the diversity
of the female form. But from my limited perspective, the curvier performers appear as tokenism.
Yes, they are sexy, and they know how to move,
but the overwhelming majority of the performers
are toned and slender. So, is having a senior citi-
zen on the stage another way to commit to the
diversity mandate? Or worse, does Nancy's an-
cient act satisfy some grandma fetish for a few
leering audience members? Would the drunk Dallas bros who frequent House of Blues heckle her?

I didn't need to worry. When Tammi True
took the stage, she was funny and self-deprecating.
She pantomimed her age. She stuck a thumb in
her mouth, taking a big breath, pretended to
magically inflate her breasts. She sauntered around
the stage, smirking. It was a burlesque of burlesque. The crowd loved it. She knew what she

was doing.

I visited Nancy a few weeks later. At this point, I had asked every question I could think of. The formal interviews drifted into friendly conversations about our families and other events. I talked about working as a writer, and trying to make ends meet. She gave me updates on the Tammi True film. She had requested a director's chair with her name on it. And she finally got it.

As I was about to leave, Nancy had a present for my wife. I told her that April loved plants but they never seemed to last long under our care. Nancy had an angel leaf begonia that she was sure could survive.

"Tell April that it's a good plant, and it will survive. She might think it's not going to, but it will."

I left her house and walked across the street to where I parked my car – encumbered by my voice recorder, steno notepad, and a huge plant. I buckled the begonia into the passenger seat.

We keep the plant in our kitchen next to the sliding glass door. Just as Nancy predicted, there were moments when I thought the plant was doomed. Most of the leaves had fallen. But sure enough, the plant restored itself with a little water and a little sunlight. As I type these words, I look over at that plant. I think of families and friends, of words on a page, of Nancy and Tammi, and of things that survive.

Acknowledgments

Thank you Tim Rogers and D Magazine, everyone at AMS Pictures especially Katie Dunn, Andy Streitfeld, Nikia Edwards, and Daniel Laabs. Thank you to the illustrious Dallas burlesque scene for their support of Tammi True and their patience with me—in particular, Shoshana Portnoy, Angi B Lovely, Pixie O'Kneel, Missy Lisa, and Ginger Valentine. Thank you Paul Milligan for a great book cover, CastingWords for untangling the hours of interviews and conversations, Kennedy for patiently doing her homework in the living room while Nancy and I talked. And always April, thank you for listening to me sort out this book, for your edits and encouragement.

—DH

This book is dedicated to my daughters Dawn and Tracy who have made this journey with me.

—NM